Magento 2 DIY

Viktor Khliupko

Apress®

Magento 2 DIY

Viktor Khliupko
Duesseldorf, Germany

ISBN-13 (pbk): 978-1-4842-2459-5   ISBN-13 (electronic): 978-1-4842-2460-1
DOI 10.1007/978-1-4842-2460-1

Library of Congress Control Number: 2016961257

Distributed to the book trade worldwide by Springer Science+Business Media New York, 233 Spring Street, 6th Floor, New York, NY 10013. Phone 1-800-SPRINGER, fax (201) 348-4505, e-mail orders-ny@springer-sbm.com, or visit www.springer.com. Apress Media, LLC is a California LLC and the sole member (owner) is Springer Science + Business Media Finance Inc (SSBM Finance Inc). SSBM Finance Inc is a **Delaware** corporation.

For information on translations, please e-mail rights@apress.com, or visit www.apress.com.

Apress and friends of ED books may be purchased in bulk for academic, corporate, or promotional use. eBook versions and licenses are also available for most titles. For more information, reference our Special Bulk Sales–eBook Licensing web page at www.apress.com/bulk-sales.

Any source code or other supplementary materials referenced by the author in this text is available to readers at www.apress.com. For detailed information about how to locate your book's source code, go to www.apress.com/source-code/.

Printed on acid-free paper

Contents at a Glance

Contents

About the Author

Viktor Khliupko is an e-commerce expert, consultant, and developer. He is also a traveler and metal music fan. He has built successful Magento-based e-commerce businesses and startups worldwide. He is the founder of the FireBear Studio.

About the Technical Reviewer

Richard Carter is a seasoned web designer and front-end developer based in the north of England. His interest in SEO comes from a desire to help clients, and fully understand the implications in the ways web sites are built with how they perform in search engines.

He lives in Newcastle upon Tyne, and is founder of established UK web design agency Peacock Carter. Richard has worked with clients including the University of Edinburgh, NHS, City & Guilds, University College Dublin, and the Scottish Government.

Acknowledgments

We've finally decided to publish our first Magento 2 book. It is its first edition, and we are going to update Magento 2 DIY when more opportunities related to the platform are available. The book in its current form consists of the following chapters:

1. Overview

2. Technology Stack

3. Resources/Tutorials/Guides

4. Installation/Download

5. Hosting

6. Composer

7. API

8. Templates

9. Extensions (New Magento 2 Modules)

10. SEO

11. Performance

12. Migration

13. Generating New Sales

14. Security

15. Certified Partners

Since the Magento 2 platform is absolutely new, the available information is not yet enough to write a book which is as informative as our Magento 1 DIY, but Magento 2 DIY is an ongoing project, so we will update the book as new information is available. Thus, having bought it, you get free lifetime updates as well as useful tips and recommendations from the Firebear team. We are going to create a manual which will cover all aspects of the platform, making it possible to master e-commerce on the basis of Magento 2 without any third-party specialists. If you are looking for a complete guide to Magento e-commerce, check our first book, Magento 1 DIY (Apress, 2016).

In addition to Magento 2 DIY, we also recommend you read the official developer documentation[1] and The Official Magento 2 User Guide[2], since they fully describe the platform. As for our book, we are going to release several more editions within this year, because the platform is constantly evolving and we get new information, which is worth sharing.

The book has been created by Viktor Khliupko[3] in collaboration with the Firebear team. Andrii Pechatkin, Demyd Maiornykov, Rita Aloshkina, Konstantin Sokolov, Oleg Pomjanski, and Andrey Nikolaev have contributed a lot to make this happen. They've shared their ideas as well as edited my thoughts. The team is:

Andrii Pechatkin[4]—lead editor, co-author;

Rita Aloshkina[5]—editor;

Demyd Maiornykov[6]—editor;

Oleg Pomjanski[7]—art direction, design;

Konstantin Sokolov[8]—consulting, editor;

Andrey Nikolaev[9]—Magento consulting;

Jewgeni Faktorov[10]—business support;

Ewgenij Sokolov—legal advisor.

The Magento platform is constantly changing, so it is impossible to create a book that will cover all its aspects. Therefore, check the Firebear blog[11] and sign up for updates. All the latest news, reviews, and advice related to both Magento 1 and Magento 2 are available there.

---

[1]http://devdocs.magento.com/
[2]http://docs.magento.com/m2/ce/user_guide/getting-started.html
[3]https://www.linkedin.com/in/bi0tech
[4]https://ua.linkedin.com/pub/andrii-pechatkin/103/bb/50a
[5]https://ua.linkedin.com/pub/rita-aloshkina/a3/1a7/a6
[6]https://ua.linkedin.com/pub/demyd-maiornykov/b5/1a4/952
[7]http://op-original.de/
[8]https://www.linkedin.com/pub/konstantin-sokolov/106/8a3/89/
[9]https://www.linkedin.com/in/andreynikolaev
[10]https://www.linkedin.com/pub/jewgeni-faktorov/105/454/55a
[11]https://firebearstudio.com/blog/

CHAPTER 1

■ ■ ■

Overview

Magento Commerce, the leading e-commerce provider, announced the general availability of much-anticipated Magento 2.0, which represents the next generation of the most popular e-commerce platform. The new product has been essentially revamped in comparison to 1.X and, as you might have guessed, it is still an open source solution with unrivaled flexibility and scalability, but with lots of new innovation opportunities. Consequently, Magento 2 empowers brands, retailers, and merchants to deliver omnichannel shopping experiences to their customers:

- quickly,
- cost-effectively,
- and with a personal approach to every buyer.

Besides, this version of the popular e-commerce platform introduces dramatic improvements in such areas as scalability, performance, and security. Thus, Magento 2.0 is a foundational milestone and an inevitable step that not only extends the company's market presence, but provides it with the status of the innovation leader and the trendsetter for the whole e-commerce ecosystem.

© Viktor Khliupko 2017
V. Khliupko, *Magento 2 DIY*, DOI 10.1007/978-1-4842-2460-1_1

Dubbed the e-commerce platform of the future, Magento 2 offers a strong competitive edge to its customers and partners, keeping their businesses ahead of the innovation curve. Since the platform relies on a revamped code base, modular architecture, and a modern technology stack, its users get the following advantages:

- quite easy, but literally unlimited customization

- fast time to market

- deployment flexibility to various cloud environments

Such features form a robust basis for exceptional business agility. Hence, the Magento 2 e-commerce changes the way you add product lines, explore new channels, and integrate additional capabilities into your web site. It not only simplifies daily processes, but features the ability to do them faster than any packaged software can.

With this release, the Magento 2 community gets rapid testing, leading omnichannel capabilities, and advanced business metrics management across all product lines and channels. Already the platform of choice among the top 1,000 internet retailers, Magento 2.0 offers the following innovations:

New architecture

As mentioned above, Magento 2 offers faster time to market, easier customization, greater code quality, and a modern technology stack. With a more modular code base as well as new service contracts, the platform provides a favorable environment for customization of default features and implementation of unique e-commerce ideas. And due to automated testing and extensive APIs, Magento 2 e-commerce means faster and higher-quality deployments and integrations to all possible third-party systems.

Better performance and scalability

While the first version of the e-commerce platform was resource-hungry and quite clumsy, the Magento 2 developers decided to improve this drawback, so the new release offers higher performance capabilities. Thus, your visitors have a great opportunity to forget about delays in accessing your e-commerce store with significantly faster page load times. And in case you are a Magento 2.0 Enterprise Edition merchant, your web site will easily handle even the largest enterprise-level site traffic and order volumes.

Revamped shopping experiences

Magento 2 introduces a revamped shopping experience which includes fast and easy checkout as well as renewed responsive design options, such as updated reference and blank themes. The streamlined checkout not only consists of fewer steps, but requires minimum information. As for the built-in new themes, they offer a seamless experience anytime, anywhere. Therefore, it doesn't matter what devices are used for shopping in the ecosystem of Magento 2.

New productivity features

First of all, we'd like to mention that Magento 2.0 introduced a new admin panel, which is more user-friendly. Another vital improvement is guided product onboarding developed with simplicity in mind. Faster import/export capabilities and customized views are also among new productivity features and options of Magento 2. All these improvements ensure that merchants will manage various types of data (such as customer, product, or order information) more efficiently. Consequently, by using Magento 2 as a major e-commerce tool, they will be able to sell the right goods to the right buyers at the proper time more precisely. And don't ignore the modular architecture, as it dramatically simplifies integrations and platform upgrades, which are planned to be published four times per year, starting from Q1 2016.

Beta Merchants

Although Magento 2 was released on November 17, there are already some beta merchants, including such giants as:

- SEAT
- Venroy
- SOL Lingerie
- Alcatel OneTouch

As you can see from the above list, Magento 2.0 has been tested across different industries. Furthermore, the platform showed good metrics along every step of the business growth cycle.

Magento 2 Extensions

It is also worth mentioning that developers have already created numerous Magento 2 extensions. There are even two modules in our portfolio:

1. The Improved Import / Export Magento 2 Extension
2. Improved Configurable Products for Magento 2

Hence, with the launch of the Magento 2 platform, the ecosystem already has a lot of useful stuff merchants need for running a successful e-commerce business. Many more Magento 2 plug-ins will be available soon.

More Magento 2 extensions are covered further in this book.

Magento 2 Courses

The company also offers courses for Magento developers. If you are planning to master the ecosystem from within, you can easily attend an online learning class. But note that some previous experience with Magento and PHP is required.

Magento 2 Migration

This is the most sensitive issue of the whole Magento 2 platform. The ecosystem offers a full data migration tool, but there are still some problems related to the transportation of customizations and extensions from 1.X to 2.0. The available solution does not provide enough features to implement a seamless migration to the next generation platform starting right now. Moreover, the absence of a robust Magento 2 migration tool is a key reasons to delay your migration to the second version of the popular e-commerce platform.

New Licensing Model

The second major Magento release introduces a tiered licensing model. The new approach provides better flexibility and aligns better to customers' further e-commerce needs. Although the revamped pricing model implementation was planned for January 1, 2016, both Community Edition and Enterprise Edition were available long before. You can find both solutions on the Magento web site: Magento 2 Community Edition and Magento 2 Enterprise Edition.

CHAPTER 2

Technology Stack

In this chapter, we provide a complete overview of the Magento 2[1] technology stack. The new version of the popular e-commerce platform has been essentially revamped, so you will discover a lot of new features and requirements in comparison with 1.X. Below, we describe all major elements of the technology stack as well as provide some useful links.

Magento 2 Technology Stack:

- PHP
- Zend Framework
- PSR-0, PSR-1, PSR-2, PSR-3, and PSR-4
- Composer
- HTML5
- CSS3 (SASS preprocessor)
- JQuery
- RequireJS
- Symfony
- Apache
- Nginx
- MySQL
- Gulp
- Twig

---

[1]https://firebearstudio.com/blog/magento-2.html

© Viktor Khliupko 2017
V. Khliupko, *Magento 2 DIY*, DOI 10.1007/978-1-4842-2460-1_2

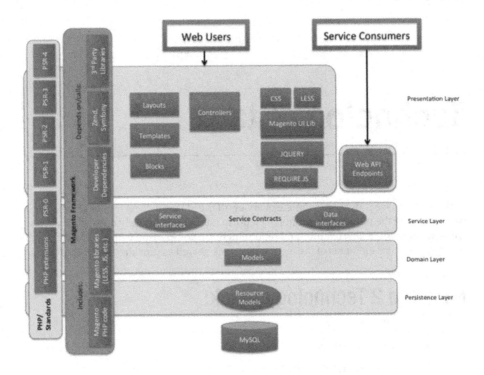

Other diagrams

PHP

Magento 2 requires PHP 5.5 and 5.6 by default. It will also work with PHP 7. The support for the new version of PHP makes the platform much faster and significantly simplifies a coding routine.

Zend Framework

Magento 2 uses bits out of different frameworks, such as Zend Framework 1, Zend Framework 2, Symfony, etc. Instead of directly relying on ZF 1, it utilizes its own adapters and interfaces used for tunneling calls to ZF 1 components. It is highly recommended to use the official Magento framework APIs to avoid problems related to the platform's internal changes.

PSR

The Magento 2 technology stack includes such coding standards as PSR-0, 1, 2, 3, and 4. PSR-0 is the default autoloading standard, PSR-1 is a set of basic coding standards, while PSR-2 is a coding style guide. Since PSR-0 has been marked as deprecated, PSR-4 is recommended as its replacement. As for PSR-3, it defines a logger interface that allows writing reusable code independent from any particular logging implementation.

Composer

Composer introduces a dependency management package for PHP. Magento 2 not only supports it out of the box, but Composer is among key system requirements of the e-commerce platform. You can check how to install Composer here.

HTML5

HTML5 is a markup language used for structuring and presenting front-end components in Magento 2. It also simplifies development and introduces new abilities, being a vital Magento 2 technology stack component.

CSS3

Instead of Bootstrap, Magento 2 uses LESS and CSS in the theme core. LESS preprocessor and LESS PHP adapter enable the use of LESS within the platform. In its turn, CSS URL resolver resolves links from CSS source files and replaces them with the correct ones. If you are wondering why Magento 2 relies on LESS instead of SASS, check this article. For further information about Magento UI library, read this post.

JQuery

JQuery is a fast, lightweight, and feature-rich JavaScript library incorporated in Magento 2 by default. The migration from Prototype to JQuery is a very important improvement related to the upgrade, since you will forget the way you were writing JavaScript in 1.X.

RequireJS

RequireJS[2] is another noticeable component of the Magento 2 technology stack related to JavaScript. Being a file and module loader optimized for in-browser use, it improves the speed and quality of your code.

---

[2]https://firebearstudio.com/blog/advanced-development-with-requirejs-magento-2-tutorial.html

Symfony

Symfony is a PHP framework and a set of reusable PHP components used in Magento 2. It speeds up your Magento 2 development by providing the ability to avoid repetitive coding tasks. YAML is a serialization standard introduced among Symfony components. It is a great format for your configuration files, since it makes them as readable as INI files and as expressive as XML files. Check this Magento 2 Yaml File and the JavaScript unit tests post for further information.

Apache

Magento 2 requires Apache 2.2.x or 2.4.x. According to a Netcraft, 60% of all web sites are using this web server, and now it is a part of the Magento 2 technology stack. You can find more information about Apache in Magento 2 here.

Nginx

Another Magento 2 technology stack component is Nginx, a reverse proxy server for such protocols as HTTPS, HTTP, POP3, SMTP, and IMAP. Besides, it is a load balancer, an HTTP cache, and an origin web server. The project is focused on high performance and concurrency as well as low usage of memory. You can discover how to use Nginx with Magento 2 here: Magento 2 Nginx Configuration[3].

MySQL

Many of the world's largest web sites have relied on MySQL for years, and now Magento also incorporates this open source database. The solution helps to save time and money powering your high-volume Magento 2 project. The e-commerce platform uses MySQL database triggers during reindexing. At the same time, Magento does not support MySQL statement-based replication.

Gulp

Although Grunt[4] is a contemporary JavaScript task runner used in Magento 2, some specialists recommend using Gulp instead of it. Gulp offers much faster building processes and streamlines deployment. It is also necessary to mention that Gulp was developed with the idea of connecting community-developed microtasks in mind, while Grunt relies on a set of commonly used tasks.

---

[3]https://firebearstudio.com/blog/magento-2-nginx-configuration.html
[4]https://firebearstudio.com/blog/magento-2-grunt.html

Twig

Twig is a fast, flexible, and secure PHP template engine supported in Magento 2. It is a Magento 2 technology stack component that will essentially simplify your work with themes and templates. You can find the Twig template engine for Magento 2 here[5]. It should be used additionally to .phtml files since it does not provide any .twig template files.

Conclusion

As you can see, the technology stack of Magento 2 looks really impressive. The platform provides a plethora of new abilities, so don't hesitate to utilize all Magento 2 features in your further e-commerce projects. In addition to the aforementioned Magento 2 technology stack components, we should also mention a native support for Redis, Varnish, and Solr. Compared to 1.x, the new opportunities are almost endless.

---

[5]https://github.com/SchumacherFM/Magento2-Twig

CHAPTER 3

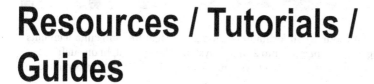

Resources / Tutorials / Guides

In this section of the Magento 2 DIY book, we've gathered the best resources about Magento 2. If you are looking for important information related to the platform, you will find the most reliable Magento 2 resources below. The full Magento 2 Developer's Resource List is published here: https://goo.gl/fpwf YP.

Learning Magento 2

First of all, we'd like to draw your attention to the Magento 2 Developer Documentation. It provides all the necessary information for getting started with the second version of the platform. Other topics are divided into groups for system administrators and developers. All Magento 2 basics are described here: Magento 2 Dev Docs[1].

Besides, there are a lot of qualified developers sharing their thoughts about Magento 2. For instance, Dale Sikkema tells about basic concepts of every Magento 2 extension on Alan Kent's blog: A MINIMAL MAGENTO 2 EXTENSION.

---

[1]http://devdocs.magento.com/

V. Khliupko, *Magento 2 DIY*, DOI 10.1007/978-1-4842-2460-1_3

Another important source of information on Magento 2 features and enhancements is Alan Storm's blog. Here—The Magento 2 Object System—he sheds light on such important aspects of Magento 2 as Object System. There are five different posts related to the topic on the blog.

The Magento 2 Object System
Articles providing a bottom up introduction to Magento 2's object manager and dependency injection system

1. Magento 2 Object Manager
2. Magento 2's Automatic Dependency Injection
3. Magento 2 Object Manager Preferences
4. Magento 2 Object Manager Argument Replacement
5. Magento 2 Object Manager Virtual Types

You can also check what Cool Ryan thinks about Magento 2. His web site is full of useful content, and there are a lot of frequent updates. Concepts and architecture, Magento 2 customization, debugging, Magento 2 modules and plug-ins, dependencies, observers, and themes are among key topics described by Ryan. You can check all this stuff here: Magento 2 by Cool Ryan.

| COOL RYAN | HOME | BLOG | MAGENTO | CONTACT |

Magento 2

There is also a dedicated category on the Inchoo blog—Magento 2 on Inchoo. You can learn more about migration, benchmarks, payment gateways, Magento 2 logging, dependency injection, and front-end architecture there.

 HOME   BLOG   WORK   SERVICES   APPROACH

In its turn, MageClass offers tutorials, screencasts, and the latest news about Magento 2. For example, you are invited to check articles about Magento 2 installation and debugging from the home page of the web site.

Welcome to MageClass

Magento2 tutorials, screencasts and up to date news.

If you have a budget for learning Magento 2, then there is an official video course called Fundamentals of Magento 2 Development. You can subscribe here. A regular price for all six units during 90 days is $689.

Other useful Magento 2 resources and blogs are:

- Karen Baker knows a lot about Magento 2 and always shares useful posts in a blog. There are some useful Magento 2 articles about migration from 1.X to 2.0. You can find all these and other materials here: Karen Baker's Blog

- It is also useful to surf on StackExchange while trying to master Magento 2. Although it is not a Magento 2 resource, there is a separate section related to the new version of the popular e-commerce platform. You can learn about Magento 2 on StackExchange here: Magento 2 tag on StackExchange.

- Max Pronko is another prominent member of the community. We've already written about him in our Real Magento Community post, and his blog is also among top learning Magento 2 resources. You can find it here: Max Pronko's Blog.

- Mage2.PRO blog offers tons of useful Magento 2 tips, tutorials, and articles by Dmitry Fedyuk. You can find all the precious Magento 2 treasures here: Mage2.PRO.

- At a certain stage of learning Magento, you will have to start practical explorations. That's where Magento 2 Sample Modules will be useful. Grab them from GitHub: Magento 2 Sample Modules.

- The Session Digital blog is also among reliable Magento 2 resources, since you can find a lot of useful articles and posts about the platform there. Hit the following link to dive deep into the world of Magento 2: Session Digital

- Nathan McBride is a certified Magento developer with a huge experience and an interesting blog. Materials related to Magento 2 are posted here: Magento 2 on Nathan McBride Blog.

- And of course we should mention the Head of Magento 2 Development and his blog among Magento 2 resources. Max Yekaterynenko knows a lot about the platform and shares his ideas here: Max Yekaterynenko's Blog

- IBNAB is another reliable source of information about the second version of the platform. The company is famous for its extensions and other Magento projects. Additionally, there is a blog on the IBNAB web site: IBNAB Blog.

- Another useful Magento 2 blog is Ash Smith's Blog.

- And don't miss Creare's Blogs and Tutorials.

- One of the important actions widely used within the Magento ecosystem is the installation of modules. You can significantly improve the default e-commerce capabilities of the platform via third-party extensions. We even have a book which describes how to turn Magento CE into Magento EE via modules. If you are not familiar with Magento 2 modules installation, check this post: How to Install Magento 2 Modules.

- For more advanced coding tips check our Magento 2 Developer's Cookbook. And don't forget about our blog: Firebear Blog.

- Other vital Magento 2 resources are: Magento 2 GitHub Repository, Magento 2 Installation Guide, Magento 2 Developer Hub, Magento 2 Documentation, Magento 2 Composer Repository, Magento 2 Sample Data and Official Magento 2 Code Samples, as well as Magento 2 Official Forum.

- All recent Magento 2 news is published here and of course on our blog.

- If you are looking for reliable Magento 2 tutorials, then we recommend you check Magento 2 tutorials by Mage World.

- And don't forget about MageInferno, since it is a very useful source of information on Magento 2.

- There is even a Magento 2 live chat among other Magento 2 resources.

- If you are looking for a request flow, here it is: Magento 2 Request Flow.

- PhpStorm Magento 2 Plugin—Magento 2 Plug-in for PHPStorm IDE used by core developers.

- Magicento—PHPStorm plug-in for Magento coders with a full description of Magento 2 installation.

- Code Migration Toolkit—tool for migrating code from Magento 1 to Magento 2.

The Real Magento Community

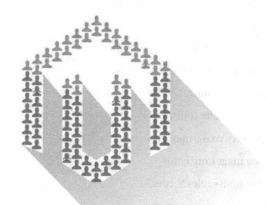

The Magento community is extremely huge. Being the most popular e-commerce solution, it gathers both developers and merchants, as well as professionals and enthusiasts. Though all this mass was disconnected in the beginning, everything has been changed within the last few years. Today, the Magento community is huge, powerful, influential, and friendly to its members, so you can always get the maximum from your interaction with it. We explain how to do this in the following post: The Power of Real Magento Community[2]. The most important resources are:

- alankent.wordpress.com/
- aschroder.com/category/magento/
- alanstorm.com/category/magento
- blog.belvg.com/category/magento-news
- atwix.com/blog/
- cyrillschumacher.com/
- bhmarks.com/blog/
- demacmedia.com/category/magento-commerce/
- eschrade.com/page/category/magento-2/
- ecomdev.org/blog

---

[2]https://firebearstudio.com/blog/the-power-of-real-magento-community.html

- excellencemagentoblog.com/
- inchoo.net/category/magento/
- fbrnc.net/
- lexiconn.com/blog/category/magento/
- magedevweekly.com/
- magebase.com/
- magenticians.com/
- nicksays.co.uk/magento/
- blog.magestore.com/
- blog.philseattlekle.com/
- solvingmagento.com/
- Demac Media
- Fishpig
- MageDaily
- Magento: The Right Way
- Magento Quickies
- Magento Tweetorials

And don't forget to check our Twitter list: Real Magento by Firebear

CHAPTER 4

■ ■ ■

Installation / Download

In this chapter, we've gathered all the necessary information about Magento 2 installation. The new version of the platform has been finally released, so don't hesitate to find out how to install the Magento 2 software. Below, we discuss different approaches to the Magento 2 installation from the use of the Setup Wizard to more complicated procedures based on Composer and the command line.

4 Types of Magento 2 Installation

Before starting our Magento 2 installation guide, we'd like to introduce you to four major approaches to this procedure. Below, you will find their descriptions as well as links to official guides. Magento 2 offers the ability to perform an easy installation and at the same time do everything to contribute code to its code base. Of course, each approach has unique requirements, so let's begin with the easiest one.

V. Khliupko, *Magento 2 DIY*, DOI 10.1007/978-1-4842-2460-1_4

Simple installation on your own server

Easy installation on your own server does not require any complicated tricks with the command line. You only need some technical expertise as well as command line access to your Magento server. This Magento 2 installation consists of the following steps:

- Download a compressed file with the Magento software.

- Then, you should extract it on your Magento server.

- Now, install the software via the Setup Wizard. Alternatively, you can rely on the command line.

Simple installation on shared hosting

This approach to the Magento 2 installation is similar to the aforementioned one. The only difference here is in the usage of shared hosting. Get ready to find a hosting provider and perform a small technical expertise. You are already familiar with the installation steps:

- Take a compressed file with the Magento software.

- Extract it on the server.

- Install the software via the Setup Wizard.

The metapackage

If you need a full control over all installed components of Magento 2, then this type of installation is for you. It is highly technical, provides access to your Magento server, and offers the ability to repackage Magento CE with other components. To install Magento 2 in such a way, do the following:

- Create a new Composer project with the list of components you want to use.

- Update your package dependencies via the same tool. Use the *composer create-project* command to get the metapackage.

- Now, you can install Magento 2 via the command line. The Setup Wizard can be utilized as well.

Cloning the Magento 2 repository

If you are a contributing developer who has a huge experience in using Composer and GitHub, then you might be interested in cloning the Magento 2 repo.

- Clone the Magento 2 repository on GitHub.

- Update package dependencies via Composer.

- Install the software. Use either the Setup Wizard or the command line.

Now, when you know four major approaches to Magento 2 installation, we can go further.

Magento 2 Installation Guide

Magento 2 System Requirements

This is the set of system requirements for Magento 2:

- Operating systems: Linux distributions (RHEL, Ubuntu, CentOS, Debian, etc.)

- The latest stable version of Composer

- Apache 2.2 or 2.4 (don't forget to enable mod_rewrite module)

- PHP: 5.4.x (x is 11 or above); 5.5.x

- PHP extensions: PDO/MySQL, mcrypt, mbstring, mhash, curl, simplexml, gd2, ImageMagick 6.3.7, soap

- MySQL 5.6.x

- SMTP server of MTA

There are some optional but also very important recommendations: php_xdebug2.2.0 or above (development environments only); PHPUnit 4.1 or above as a tool for the command line.

Composer and Magento

To install the Magento software, you now need a Composer. It provides you with the ability to manage the system, extensions, and dependencies. The key features of Composer are:

- It enables you to reuse third-party libraries with no need to bundle them with source code.

- With Composer, you get a component-based architecture with a robust dependency management.

- The tool manages dependencies; as a result you get much less compatibility issues and conflicts between extensions.

- You also get versioned dependencies with Composer.

- And don't forget about Semantic versioning.

- Last but not least is that Composer supports PHP Framework Interoperability standard.

More information is available in our Magento 2 Composer Guide[1].

Composer Installation

- Create a new and empty directory on a Magento server.

- Enter the following:

```
1   curl -sS https://getcomposer.org/installer | php
2   mv composer.phar /usr/local/bin/composer
```

There are also some additional installation options, you can find them in Composer installation documentation.

- Restart Apache: for Ubuntu use *service apache2 restart*; for CentOS use: *service httpd restart*

Magento GitHub Repository Cloning

- It is extremely important to use secure shell (SSH): generate SSH keys; add a public key to GitHub.

- Copy the HTTPS clone URL or Magento GitHub repository SSH to the clipboard.

- Open Magento GitHub repository in a browser.

---

[1]https://firebearstudio.com/blog/magento-2-composer.html

- Click SSH or HTTPS (under the "Clone URL" field on the right side).

- Use "Copy to clipboard" button.

This is the example of HTTPS clone URL:

- Change the docroot directory of web server: for Ubuntu, it's */var/www*; for CentOS - */var/www/html*.

- Use one of the following commands:

- For HTTPS: *git clone https://github.com/magento/magento2.git*

- For SSH: *git clone git@github.com:magento/magento2.git*

- Now the repository will be cloned on a server.

File System Permissions & Ownership

The recommend settings for permissions are:

- **700 permissions for all directories (drwx—-)**. The owner gets the full control—the ability to read/write/execute; other users have no permissions.

- **600 permissions for all files (-rw—-)**. The owner is able to read and write, but nobody else gets the permissions.

Now, when the user of a web server owns the Magento 2 file system, you should use the following:

- Use *cd magento2* to change the Magento directory.

- Use *ps -ef | grep apache2* to find the web server user in Ubuntu; *grep User /etc/httpd/conf/httpd.conf-* in CentOS.

- Use *chown -R [your web server user name]* to set ownership; in CentOS - *chown -R apache*; in Ubuntu - *chown -R www-data*.

And finally you can set the permissions:

```
1   find . -type d -exec chmod 700 {} \;
2   find . -type f -exec chmod 600 {} \;
```

Installation Dependencies Update

Magento installation dependencies—Introduction
    Magento relies on Composer for the first time, so before installing any Magento software, you must set up the Composer and perform the following:

- First of all you have to Install the Composer.

- Now you must Switch to the Apache user to let the Composer write files to the docroot of web server as the correct user.

- From both of the below directories, run the composer install command:

```
1   <your Magento install dir>
2   <your Magento install dir>/setup
```

Keep in mind, that the main reason for failure is an incomplete or non-functional installation.

Switching to the Apache user:

For both Ubuntu and CentOS, avoid running Composer as the root user. And don't forget that the user of web server on CentOS is *apache*; on Ubuntu - *www-data*.

Ubuntu

- Enter *su www-data*.

- In case you don't know the user's password and a dedicated prompt appears, continue with the next step.

Use the following commands to enable the *www-data user's shell* and to set a password:

```
1   sudo chsh -s /bin/bash www-data
2   sudo passwd www-data
```

- Run *su www-data* again and enter the password.

- To end the procedure, continue with Running Composer to update dependencies.

CentOS

- Run *su - apache*. If "This account is currently not available" error displays, continue with the next step.

- Use *sudo chsh -s /bin/bash apache* to give apache a valid shell account.

- Enter *su - apache* again—it should work now.

Running Composer to update dependencies

- Switch or log in as the web server user to the Magento server.

- Change to the installation directory of Magento 2 - *cd /var/www/ html/magento2*

- Run *composer install* to update package dependencies.

Magento Software Installation With The Setup Wizard

Running the Setup Wizard

With the Setup Wizard, you can go back and forward through the pages of installation. You can't skip pages, and you have to enter all the required information before you can go to the next step. It is possible to run the installer again or return to a previous page to fix errors.

Getting started

- Open a web browser.

- Enter *http://[Magento host or IP]/[path to Magento root]/setup* in the location or address bar. For the Magento server's IP address "192.0.2.10" and magento2 directory, you should enter *http://192.0.2.10/magento2/setup*

- Click Agree and Set Up Magento.

- To complete the installation, continue with the following sections.

Step 1: Readiness Check

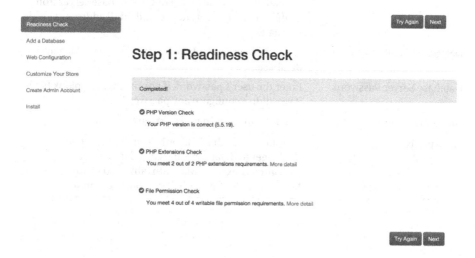

- Use Start Readiness Check option.

- Resolve all the problems if there are any before you go to the next step.

- Use More detail to see the additional information about each check.

- Click Next.

Step 2: Add a Database

Item	Description
Database Server Host	Enter localhost for the web and database servers located on the same host. For the database server from a different host, use its fully qualified IP address or hostname.
Database Server Username	Enter the username of the instance owner of Magento database.
Database Server Password	Enter the user's password, if any or leave the blank field if you didn't configure any password.
Database Name	Enter the instance name of Magento database.
Table prefix	You should use this field only if you're installing the Magento database tables in a database instance with already existing Magento tables. To identify the Magento tables for this installation, use a prefix.

Step 3: Web Configuration

Item	Description
Your Store Address	Enter the URL of your storefront. It should include scheme and trailing slash (http://www.example.com/).
Magento Admin Address	Enter the URL of your Magento Admin.

Optionally, click Advanced Options and enter the following information:

Item	Description
HTTPS Options	To enable the use of SSL in the indicated URL, select the checkbox. Do this only if your web server supports SSL.
Apache Rewrites	Select this check box only if you enabled server rewrites while Apache installation.
Encryption Key	Magento can generate an encryption key. Use I want to use a Magento generated key option to receive it. If you have your own encryption key, you should use I want to use my own encryption key.

Step 4: Customize Your Store

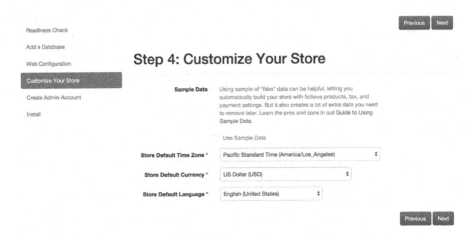

- Use Store Default Time Zone list to set the time zone of your store.
- Use Store Default Currency list to choose the default currency.
- Use Store Default Language list to choose the default language.

Step 5: Create Admin Account

Item	Description
New Username	Enter a username with which you will log in to the Admin of your Magento store. You will be an administrator and will be able to create other users and administrative users under this username.
New E-Mail	This is the field for e-mail address of Magento administrator.
New Password	The field for the password of administrator.
Confirm Password	Password confirmation field.

Step 6: Install

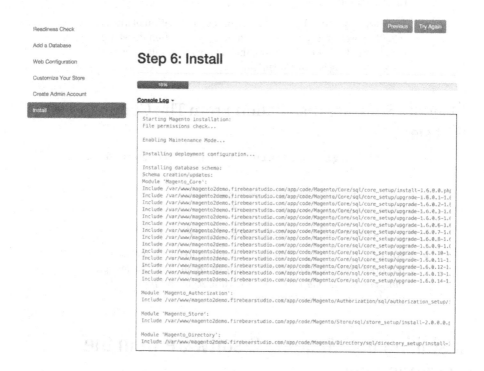

Click Install Now and you will get the following options:

- By clicking Console Log, you will be able to see installation progress and error details.

- By clicking Previous in the event of problems, you will be able to go back to fix incorrect entries.

- By clicking Try Again, you will be able to run the installation again.

If the installation was successful, you will see the message Success.

Viewing the installation log

The Setup Wizard creates **install.log**, a log file, which can be useful for the debugging or in the actions verification. To locate the log, you should:

- Use a text editor to open php.ini. If you don't know where php.ini is located:

- Switch to or log in as or the web server user.

- In the docroot of your web server, create phpinfo.php.

- Use a web browser to access phpinfo.php.

- You can find the location of php.ini specified as Loaded Configuration File.

- Find **sys_temp_dir**. Its value determines the location of install. log. PHP uses that value as its default in a case when the value is commented out. Keep in mind, that a typical default value is /tmp, so the log is /tmp/install.log.

Magento Software Installation From The Command Line
First steps

- You should log in to the Magento server as the web server user or you can switch.

- Change **cd <your Magento install dir>/setup**: *cd /var/www/ magento2/setup* for Ubuntu and *cd*

- */var/www/html/magento2/setup* for CentOS

- You can also use the following commands to find some values for required options: *php -f index.php help language* for Language; *php -f index.php help timezone* for Time zone and *php -f index. php help currency* for Currency.

Installing the Magento 2 software from the command line

Magento 2 Dev Beta—Installation with CLI.
   The install command follows the next format:

```
1    php -f index.php install --[installation option name]=[installation
     option value]
```

Name	Value	Required?
base_url	Use Base URL to access your Magento Admin and storefront in the format http[s]://[host or ip]/ [your Magento base dir]/. A scheme and a slash are required. [your Magento base dir] is the docroot-relative path, where the Magento software will be installed. It can be magento2 or might be blank. Use http://localhost/ [your Magento base dir]/ or http://127.0.0.1/ [your Magento base dir]/ to access Magento on localhost.	Yes
backend_frontname	This is the path to access the Magento Admin. It is is appended to Base URL. For the Base URL http:// www.example.com and the Admin Pat admin, the Admin Panel's URL would be is http://www. example.com/admin	Yes
db_host	You can use the database server's fully qualified hostname, IP address, localhost if your database web servers are on the same host, or UNIX socket (/var/ run/mysqld/mysqld.sock). In addition, there is an option to specify the database server port in its host name: www.example.com:9000	Yes
db_name	This is the name of the Magento database instance where you are going to install the Magento database tables.	Yes
db_user	Magento database instance owner's username.	Yes
db_pass	The password of Magento database instance owner.	No
db_prefix	Use it if you have more than one Magento instance running on a server with all tables in the same database.	No
admin_firstname	First name of Magento administrator user.	Yes
admin_lastname	Last name of Magento administrator user.	Yes
admin_email	E-mail address of Magento administrator user.	Yes
admin_username	Username of Magento administrator.	Yes
admin_password	Password of Magento administrator user.	Yes
language	Language code for the Admin and storefront. To view the list of language codes enter php -f index.php help language from the setup directory.	Yes
currency	Default currency - php -f index.php help currency from the setup directory.	Yes

(*continued*)

31

Name	Value	Required?
timezone	Default time zone - php -f index.php help time zone from the setup directory.	Yes
use_secure	1 enables the use of SSL in all URLs (your web server should support SSL). 0 disables the use of SSL.	No
base_secure_url	1 - SSL is preferred in Magento URLs. 0 - SSL is not used.	No
use_secure_admin	1 - SSL is used to access the Magento Admin.0 - SSL is not used with the Admin.	No
admin_use_ security_key	1 - Magento software uses a randomly generated key value to access different pages in the Admin and forms. 0 disables the feature.	No
session_save	Use files to store session data in the file system; db.files—in the database.	No
key	Specify a key to encrypt data in the Magento database or Magento will generate its own.	No
cleanup_database	Specify this parameter without a value to drop database tables before Magento software installation, or the Magento database will be left intact.	No
db_init_statements	This is the advanced parameter for MySQL configuration. To set any values use this this link— you will find all the necessary information there.	No
sales_order_ increment_prefix	Set a string value, which will be used as a prefix for sales orders. As a result, the payment processor will be provided with unique order number.	No

Sample localhost installation

As a result of such installation, your Magento receives the following options:

- The software is installed in the magento2 directory. Your storefront URL - http://localhost/magento2; Magento Admin - http://localhost/magento2/admin;

- The database and web server are on the same host.

- The database name, username and password are magento.

- The properties of Magento administrator includes:

- Both first and last name are Magento User.

- Username - *admin*, the password - *iamtheadmin*

- E-mail address - *user@example.com*

- The default language is U.S. English.

- The currency is U.S. dollars.

- The time zone is U.S. Central.

```
1  php -f index.php install --base_url=http://localhost/magento2/
2  --backend_frontname=admin
3  --db_host=localhost --db_name=magento --db_user=magento
   --db_pass=magento
4  --admin_firstname=Magento --admin_lastname=User
   --admin_email=user@example.com
5  --admin_username=admin --admin_password=iamtheadmin --language=en_US
6  --currency=USD --timezone=America/Chicago
```

- Enter this command as a single line.

Reinstalling the Magento software

- Delete and re-create the database instance (you can do it optionally).

- Log in to your server as a user who has permission to modify files in the file system of Magento.

- Run the following commands:

```
1  cd <your Magento install dir>
2  git pull
3  composer install
4  cd setup
5  composer install
```

- Repeat all the sections about Magento installation from the command line.

Magento 2 sample data

Now when you are logged as the Magento file system owner, you can install the Magento 2 sample data via the command line:

```
php <your Magento install dir>/bin/magento sampledata:deploy
```

Please note that it is necessary to authenticate to complete the action. If you see the following authentication error

```
[Composer\Downloader\TransportException]
```

The 'https://repo.magento.com/packages.json' URL required authentication. You must be using the interactive console to authenticate.

It is necessary to change to your Magento 2 installation directory and then run the following command:

```
composer update
```

Please note that it will prompt you for your authentication keys.

Magento 2 Setup Verification

Open a web browser and go to your storefront. If the browser displays the same storefront page, your installation was a success.

Default welcome msg!   My Account   My Wish List   Register   Log In

Magento
an ebay inc company

Search entire store here...   🔍   🛒

Advanced Search

Home Page

CMS homepage content goes here.

Verify the Magento 2 Admin

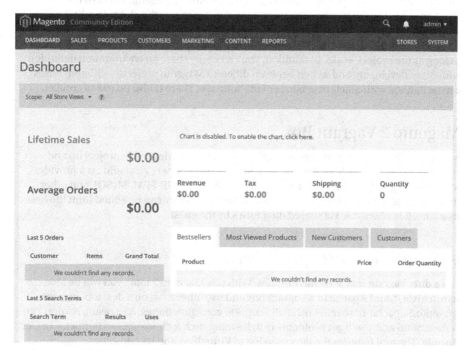

Use the same browser to open Magento 2 Admin, and log in as a Magento Administrator. If your Admin looks like a sample Magento 2 Admin page, then your installation was successfull.

How To Create A Virtual Machine For Magento 2

Since Magento 2 requires MySQL 5.6, there are a lot of problems with running Magento 2 in environments such as MAMP and XAMPP with MySQL 5.5 support only. If you are going to switch between Magento 1 and 2 projects, the issue can turn into a serious headache. Below, we've gathered information about solving the versions problem with the help of Magento 2 virtualization.

The traditional form of virtualization requires such software as VirtualBox on a host OS. A Virtual Machine (VM) with its OS runs inside this software. The other form relies on Linux containers, which are used by Docker. They use Linux OS features like chroot to guarantee a set of processes in one "container." With this form of virtualization, you don't have to run a full new OS. Different containers are able to run different versions of software.

Vagrant is a special tool designed to create and configure development environments. Vagrant provides few ways of usage. Firstly, Magento 2 code base is checked out in the file system, whereupon the developer gets the ability to edit the code with the help of text editors. Secondly, the web browser is run right on the OS. Thirdly, the code resides in a Vagrant box. The content of the box doesn't matter much to a developer, as long as the project works. In addition, you can easily share an environment definition with other developers and switch between different Magento projects—different boxes can be defined with different versions of the software. There is also no risk of conflict.

Magento 2 Vagrant Box

Magento 2 Vagrant Box[2] provides a simple way to get your Magento 2 project up and running. Based on a Debian Wheezy box provided via Puppet (VirtualBox is a provider), Magento2 Vagrant Box installs Apache 2 +FastCGI, PHP, PHP-FPM, MySQL and other dependencies. Being a git submodule, Magento 2 repository can be edited from the host machine. It is accessible via shared directories by the guest.

vagrant magento2 apache base

Get a dirty Vagrant image within minutes. With this Magento 2 tool[3], you will be able to run MySQL and Apache in a Vagrant box and use other tools on a desktop. vagrant-magento2-apache-base relies on shell scripts to configure things. As a result, readers can poke around and you'll get problems with learning such technologies as Puppet, Chef, or Ansible. The tool requires the latest version of VirtualBox and its Add-ons.

How to Install Magento 2 with Docker

Get your ticket to the world of containerization with Docker. In a situation where you are working with several projects, which run on different software versions (for example Magento 1.x on PHP 5.4, Magento 2.x on PHP 5.6, and web host on PHP 5.3) you probably face the problem when system packages don't exactly match each other. Therefore, you can use Docker to simplify interactions with all your projects. This software solution allows you to package your apps with all their dependencies into standardized units (containers) designed for convenient software development, since they wrap up everything into a complete filesystem with runtime, code, system tools and libraries. As a result, a package runs the same in all possible environments. To get deeper insights into what is Docker, check this page[4] on the official web site of the software. I also recommend you get acquainted with basic aspects of Magento development with Docker here[5]. Additionally, there is an important article on Magento 2 development with Docker on OS X[6] on

---

[2]https://github.com/rgranadino/mage2_vagrant
[3]https://github.com/alankent/vagrant-magento2-apache-base
[4]https://www.docker.com/whatisdocker
[5]http://coderoncode.com/2015/03/05/getting-started-with-magento-and-docker.html
[6]http://mageinferno.com/blog/magento-2-development-docker-os-x

Mageinferno. Another important source of useful information related to Magento 2 and Docker is Alan Kent's blog. For instance, he describes how to reduce install headaches with the aid of virtualization here[7]. Hit this link[8] to get Docker on your computer.

PHP 7 Docker Image for Magento 2

The magento2-php[9] image contains PHP configurations for Magento 2. Besides PHP 7, it also includes 5.6-fpm.

If you have any questions, check the official Magento 2 CE User Gide[10]. The manual consists of three major parts: Contents, Introduction, and Basic Configuration. Although there is a Contents section on the first page of the Magento Community Edition 2.0 User Guide, there is also a dedicated section in the manual which provides more information by showing additional topics.

In its turn, the Introduction section describes available Magento resources, discusses the installation process, and shows how to access a Magento account. Besides, it sheds light on the main pages and key features of a Magento 2 web site. As for the Basic Configuration section, it introduces the Admin along with basic configuration settings and best practices. Besides, there is a "How To Use This Guide" section in a manual. Additionally, you can use its PDF version.

---

[7]http://alankent.me/2014/12/21/reducing-magento-2-install-pain-through-virtualization/

[8]https://hub.docker.com/search/?q=magento2&page=1&isAutomated=0&isOfficial=0&starCount=0&pullCount=0

[9]https://hub.docker.com/r/mageinferno/magento2-php/

[10]http://docs.magento.com/m2/ce/user_guide/getting-started.html

CHAPTER 5

■ ■ ■

Hosting

Since Magento 2 introduces a bunch of brand-new features and improvements, it also has updated requirements related to hosting. Hence, solutions optimized for 1.X are no longer suitable for the new version of the e-commerce platform. Although they can still work with Magento 2, 1.X optimized hostings never provide the highest possible performance. That's why we'd like to describe Magento 2 hosting services, but let's discuss new system requirements first.

Magento 2 System Requirements

- Nginx—Magento 2 supports Nginx by default.

- PHP 7 is going to make the platform lightning fast.

- Composer is now a part of the system.

- Varnish—heavily consumed APIs and dynamic web sites are no longer a problem for Magento.

V. Khliupko, *Magento 2 DIY*, DOI 10.1007/978-1-4842-2460-1_5

- Redis—top-notch performance of Magento 2 is now achieved with the advanced key-value cache.

- MySQL—the most popular open source database for web apps is also on board.

- PHPUnit and XDebug are now required for your dev server.

As you can see, there are a lot of new features which require a special approach when it comes to hosting Magento 2. To get a deeper insight into the new conditions, check this article: Magento 2 System Requirements[1]. The understanding of system requirements will help you choose Magento 2 hosting, which will fully satisfy the needs of the platform. Please note that a hosting server should support all of them:

Magento 2 Hosting Requirements

- I should run the latest available PHP and MySQL versions.

- The SSH access is another important feature, since it provides the ability to use the Magento 2 CLI and Composer.

- As you might have guessed, an optimized Magento 2 web hosting server should support Composer.

- Varnish is also a must.

We recommend you check reviews of a Magento 2 hosting service you choose and compare it with system requirements you have. Thus, you will be able to get a Magento 2 web hosting which fully complies with your business needs and Magento 2 system requirements

Here at Firebear, we anticipate that all major Magento hosting partners will provide reliable hosting options for Magento 2 as well. For example, Nexcess and RackSpace have always offered various robust solutions optimized for the e-commerce platform, therefore you can monitor the below companies:

- Nexcess[2]

- Rackspace[3]

- Hetzner[4]

- Site5[5]

---

[1]https://firebearstudio.com/blog/magento-2-system-requirements.html
[2]https://www.nexcess.net/
[3]http://www.rackspace.com/
[4]https://www.hetzner.de/en/
[5]https://www.site5.com/p/magento/

- Simple Helix[6]
- Aspiration Hosting[7]
- CloudWays[8]
- RackSpeed[9]
- SimpleServers[10]

---

[6]http://www.simplehelix.com/managed-hosting/magento-hosting
[7]http://www.aspirationhosting.com/magento-hosting/
[8]http://www.cloudways.com/blog/host-magento-2-on-cloud/
[9]https://rackspeed.de/magento-2-hosting/
[10]https://www.simpleservers.co.uk/magento-2-hosting

CHAPTER 6

■ ■ ■

Composer

In this chapter, we will explain how to use the application-level package manager with the most popular e-commerce platform. Being inspired by Node.js npm, Composer provides a unified format that simplifies dependency management of PHP software. The usage of Composer in various Magento 2 projects is inevitable, because it is a part of the platform. You can run the package manager through the command line, installing dependencies for your modules. Besides, Composer provides the ability to install Magento 2 extensions available on Packagist (the repo is described below). Another important feature introduced in Composer is a set of autoload capabilities for libraries that essentially simplifies the usage of third-party software solutions.

Magento 2 Composer Integration

You must install Composer if you use the Magento software. The package manager will be necessary to update Magento 2 and its components, even if you've installed the e-commerce solution from an archive.

The Magento 2 Composer combination offers the following features:

- provides the ability to use third-party libraries while you don't have to bundle them with source code of Magento 2

- offers a component-based architecture as well as reliable dependency management

- reduces extension conflicts as well as various compatibility issues

- streamlines your work with versioned dependencies

- introduces semantic versioning

- supports some useful standards, such as PHP Framework Interoperability

In its turn, Magento 2 relies on Composer while packaging different components as well as product editions. Since some third party components used by Magento are not presented in the code base, they exist in a form of dependencies in composer.json files. Below, we will shed light on them.

© Viktor Khliupko 2017
V. Khliupko, *Magento 2 DIY*, DOI 10.1007/978-1-4842-2460-1_6

Magento 2 and composer.json

While talking about **composer.json** files, it is necessary to explain what is a package. A package is a directory which contains composer.json as well as other component files. It's an inevitable component of the Magento 2 Composer tandem. These are the types of composer.json packages:

- Root composer.json package includes the main composer.json file utilized for declaring dependencies on third-party components and used as a template for other root composer.json files. It is located under composer.json, its naming convention is magento/magento2ce, its type is project.

- CE project composer.json package represents Magento CE project and declares dependencies on the class autoloader and the magento product. It is located under composer.json, its naming convention is magento/project-community-edition, its type is project.

- CE product composer.json package represents Magento CE product and declares dependencies on such Magento components as themes and modules as well as third-party components. The package is located under composer.json, its naming convention is magento/project-community-edition, its type is metapackage.

- base composer.json package represents Magento CE base package which includes files/directories (excluding components) as well as introduces the "require" section to list the latter. The package is located under composer.json, its naming convention is magento/magento2-base, its type is magento2-component.

- module shows a fully qualified name of a module, which is broken down into vendor, suffixes that represent the rest of the words, and the mandatory prefix. The package is located under app/code/Magento/<Module>/composer.json, its naming conventions are magento/module-catalog-inventory and magento/module-checkout, its type is magento2-module.

- theme belongs to areas, that's why you should use the area name as the first suffix. The package is located under app/design/<area>/Magento/<theme>/composer.json, its naming conventions are magento/theme-frontend-blank and magento/theme-adminhtml-backend, its type is magento2-theme.

- language packs package require the lowercase language identifier. The package is located under app/i18n/magento/<language>/composer.json, its naming conventions are magento/language-en_us, magento/language-de_de, etc., its type is magento2-language.

- Magento framework/libraries contains only one package— magento/framework. Particular libraries are not distinguished as separate components. The package is located under lib/internal/ Magento/Framework/composer.json, its naming convention is magento/framework, its type is magento2-library.

The Magento 2 Composer cooperation provides you with the ability to submit the following package types to Magento Connect:

- magento2-module usually includes source files and the top composer.json.

- metapackage is a placeholder that gathers a collection of packages.

- magento2-theme package type is utilized with theme packages.

- magento2-language usually contains a .csv file used for translating certain content.

Naming conventions in Magento 2 and Composer

The required format for Composer packages in Magento 2 is:

```
1   <vendor_name>/<package_name>
```

Please note that there is a requirement for all letters in the name in the Magento 2 Composer duo—they must be lowercase.

Hence, Magento packages are named according to the following format:

```
1   magento/*
```

If a package name consists of several words, these word should be separated with dash according to the Composer specification. The Magento package name convention looks as follows:

```
1   magento/<type-prefix>-<suffix>[-<suffix>]...
```

- *type-prefix* is a component type in a Magento-specific domain.

- *suffix* is something that identifies the component within its type.

Package Types

Each component of Magento 2 can be categorized into one of eight types listed above. In case you have a component that doesn't fit into any specific category, you can generalize it to magento-component.

With the aid of identifier types related to each component, the Magento 2 system arranges both directories and files of each component and places them in correct locations according to the available directory structure of Magento 2.

How to Install Composer

The following section of our Magento 2 Composer guide describes how to install Composer. First of all, you should check whether the software solution is already installed or not. Open a command prompt and enter this command:

```
1   composer --help
```

If the command displays the appropriate information, you've already installed Composer. If you see an error, perform the following actions:

- Go to your Magento server and create a new empty there.

- Run the commands listed below:

```
1   curl -sS https://getcomposer.org/installer | php
2   mv composer.phar /usr/local/bin/composer
```

Congratulations! You've just installed Composer on Magento 2. If you have any questions, see the official Composer installation guide.

How to Deploy Magento 2 CE with Composer

To deploy Magento 2 CE with Composer, use the following command:

```
1   git clone https://github.com/magento/magento2 ./magento2
2   composer install
```

If you want to update your Magento 2 project to the latest available version, utilize this command:

```
1   git pull composer install
```

If you are going to deploy Magento 2 CE through Composer to the web site root, which is /var/www/example.com/htdocs, there can be two different conditions: you can be inside or outside the deploying directory performing the appropriate Magento 2 Composer command. In the first case, run this one:

```
1   cd /var/www/example.com/htdocs
2   composer create-project "magento/project-community-edition"
```

In the second case, utilize this one:

```
1   composer create-project "magento/project-community-edition" /var/www/
example.com/htdocs
```

Source

How to clone the Magento 2 repository via Composer

This Magento 2 Composer procedure is necessary if you are going to contribute to the code base of the platform. You can choose between the master or develop branches. The first one is more stable and you can clone it with the help of the optional [-b master] argument, while the second one is the latest and and it will be cloned by default. You can find the full description of the procedure here: (Contributor) Clone the Magento repository.

How to package a module in Magento 2

In Magento 2, Composer packages are used for distributing, installing, and upgrading modules. To package your module, it is necessary to:

- create a composer.json file;
- package and then publish a module on the Magento Connect.

Magento 2 Composer file

composer.json defines such basic information as name, version, and requirements. Use only a root directory of a module to place its composer.json file and pay attention to the Composer generic schema and the following restrictions:

- name—requires using the **<vendor-name>/module-<module-name>** format as well as lowercase letters only. Dashes must be used to separate words in the **<module-name>**.

- type—set this value to magento2-module for all your modules.

- autoload—specifies important data to be loaded. For further information, check Composer Autoloading.

Metapackages

While talking about the Magento 2 Composer integration, it is necessary to pay special attention to metapackages, since they provide the ability to create an extension that consists of several packages, combining it into a cohesive system. A metapackage is a .zip file that contains the metapackage composer.json file only. If your extension uses more than one package, use a metapackage as its root package. Note that it is the only use case for this package type. For further information, check the official composer.json documentation.

An ordinary composer.json metapackage file looks as follows:

```
1   {
2   "name": "magento/sample-data",
3   "version": "1.0.0-beta",
4   "type": "metapackage",
5   "require": {
6   "magento/module-sample-data": "self.version",
7   "magento/sample-data-media": "~0.42.0-beta2",
8   },
9   "autoload": {
10  "files": [ "registration.php" ],
11  "psr-4": {
12  "Magento\\sample-data": ""
13  }
14  }
15  }
```

As for a composer.json file for a module, it has the following structure:

```
1   {
2   "name": "magento/sample-module-newpage",
3   "description": "A Magento 2 module that creates a new page",
4   "type": "magento2-module",
5   "version": "1.0.0",
```

```
 6    "license": [
 7    "OSL-3.0",
 8    "AFL-3.0"
 9    ],
10    "require": {
11    "php": "~5.5.0|~5.6.0|~7.0.0",
12    "magento/framework": "~1.0.0"
13    },
14    "autoload": {
15    "files": [ "registration.php" ],
16    "psr-4": {
17    "Magento\\SampleNewPage\\": ""
18    }
19    }
20    }
```

Packaging and publishing extensions

The Magento 2 Composer combination requires the following steps to be performed in order to package and publish your extensions:

1. First of all, create a package of your module via a zip operation. Unnecessary directories should be excluded. Use dashes to separate words and alphanumeric characters to set the package file name. Please note that it is important not to use whitespaces.

2. It is also worth mentioning that the Magento 2 system can retrieve your package from any valid URL of GitHub or other third-party repo.

GitHub and Packagist

If you are going to work with GitHub and Packagist, do the following things:

1. If you are planning to host your extension package on GitHub and Packagist, set up git on your machine.

2. Then, navigate to your module directory, it should have composer.json in the root, and turn it into a new git repository. For further information, check this GitHub documentation.

3. Now, when your module is pushed on GitHub, you can refer to it directly via Composer or do the same action through Packagist:

    • Create an account on Packagist.

    • Find the Submit Package button, click it, and paste your GitHub repository link there.

Private repositories

As for private repositories, they can be used for private code or development. At the same time, it is necessary to perform installation of such modules via a CLI. The Magento 2 Composer tandem sets the following requirements:

1. Use Satis or Toran to make your packaging repository.

2. Create a package and submit or register it on your repository.

3. Add the following code to your composer.json:

```
1  {
2  "repositories": [
3  {
4  "type": "composer",
5  "url": [repository url here]
6  }
7  ]
8  }
```

Now, you can use the require field to reference all your packages from the private repository.

For more information on creating Magento 2 Composer packages, follow this link: CREATING A MAGENTO 2 COMPOSER MODULE by Alan Kent.

Source

Useful Links

- Core Magento 2 Composer packages

- Magento 2 extensions on Packagist—the main Composer repository

- Composer

CHAPTER 7

■ ■ ■

API

The following section of the Magento 2 DIY book sheds light on the Magento 2 API, so let's explain what this term means. Application program interface is a special interface which consists of protocols, routines, and tools designed to simplify the process of software development. Since APIs' major purpose is to specify how different software parts interact within a system, they are often used to program graphical user interface components. Good APIs provide all building blocks necessary for developing an application, so a programmer only has to put them together. Although Magento 2 APIs incorporate the same principle, there are tons of nuances related to the e-commerce platform. So, what is the Magento 2 API?

© Viktor Khliupko 2017

V. Khliupko, *Magento 2 DIY*, DOI 10.1007/978-1-4842-2460-1_7

Magento 2 API Framework

We will start our journey into the world of the Magento 2 API with core features of the Magento web API framework, since it provides developers with the means to use web services connected with the Magento 2 system. If you are trying to master the Magento 2 API you should know that:

- the system supports both REST and SOAP APIs;

- you'll have to deal with three types of authentication: OAuth 1.0a for third-party apps, tokens for mobile apps, and login credentials for admins and customers;

- accounts and integrations are assigned to resources if there is access to them; the API framework checks whether a call is authorized to perform the request;

- you only need a few lines of xml to configure any Magento or third-party service as a web API; all XML elements and attributes should be defined in a webapi.xml file, otherwise a service will not be exposed;

- the Magento 2 API framework relies on two models—CRUD and search, but does not support web hooks;

- it offers the web API responses field filtering for conserving mobile bandwidth;

- since Magento 2 APIs utilize integration style, a single web API call can run multiple services simultaneously.

Magento 2 API Opportunities

The Magento 2 APIs provide the ability to perform a wide array of tasks. For example, you can create a mobile app for your customers or employees. There is also an opportunity to integrate your e-commerce store with CRM or ERP systems with the help of Magento 2 APIs as well as connect a Magento 2 web site with a CMS. Besides, you can develop JavaScript widgets for both storefronts and admin panels.

Getting Started With Magento 2 API

First of all, it is necessary to register a new web service on your Magento admin. In case of token-based authentication, create a new web service user under System/All Users/Add New User. For session-based and OAuth authentication, there is no need to do this.

Then, create a new integration under System/Integration/Add New Integration. Please note that it is extremely important to set up resources the integration can access.

The final step requires using a REST or SOAP client for further configuration.

API Integration in the Magento 2 back end looks as follows:

System/Integration:

Integration Info

Available APIs

Stores/Configuration/Services/Magento Web API and OAuth:

Magento Web API

OAuth

Magento 2 REST API

Based on the HTTP protocol, Magento 2 REST API interactions incorporate functions aimed at making requests and receiving responses. The caller issues an HTTP request with the following elements:

- an HTTP header (for authentication and other instructions);

- a verb (GET, PUT, POST, or DELETE);

- an endpoint (URI that determines three important components: the server, the web service, and the acted resource);

- a call payload (all input attributes and parameters supplied with the request).

Please note that Magento 2 returns both a response payload and an HTTP status code. For further information about Magento 2 REST API, check the following official guides:

- Authentication

- Construct a request

- Use cURL to run the request

- Review the response

Magento 2 REST API Reference

Magento 2 Community Edition offers a set of REST APIs which are listed here. To generate live REST API documentation, install Swagger UI on your server. With the following link, you will be able to generate a JSON schema with third-party modules and extension attributes from your system: http://<magento_- host>/rest/default/schema.

After generating the schema file, you should load it into your Swagger UI. You can find all REST schema endpoints for available services here.

Magento 2 SOAP API Reference

You can find the official Magento 2 SOAP API reference here: SOAP Reference. It provides a list of service names per each module. The SOAP WSDL endpoint format looks as follows:

```
1   http://<magento_host>/soap/<store_code>?wsdl&services=<serviceName1,ser
viceName2,..>
```

Magento 2 and Swagger

If you don't want to read a 31,000-line JSON document, pay attention to Swagger, since it generates a more human-friendly version of the schema by defining the JSON document format. Follow this link to check the official demo by Swagger. For further information on Swagger and Magento 2, examine this article: MAGENTO 2 REST API SWAGGER SCHEMA.

CHAPTER 8

Templates

In this chapter, we will gather popular Magento 2 templates and themes. In addition, you will find some useful information on theme development in Magento 2, key aspects of the Magento 2 front-end architecture, as well as other features related to the Magento 2 theming.

Magento 2 Templates and Themes

We constantly update the list of Magento 2 themes here: Magento 2 Templates and Themes[1]. You can find top solutions in the post. Besides, there are a lot of individual reviews of each theme listed there, so check further links to our blog.

---

[1]https://firebearstudio.com/blog/magento-2-templates.html

V. Khliupko, *Magento 2 DIY*, DOI 10.1007/978-1-4842-2460-1_8

Ketty Magento 2 Beta

Ketty Magento 2 Beta was among the first Magento 2 themes available for the platform. In addition to perfect look, it offers such features as responsive design, cross-browser support, slider, configurable swatches, Ajax cart, product zoom, improved checkout, and a user-friendly admin panel. This Magento 2 theme is free, you only have to pay with a tweet.

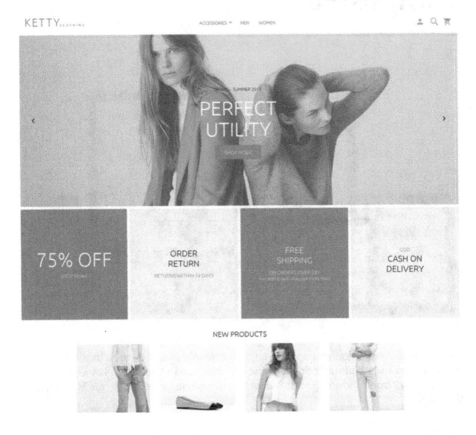

Get Ketty Magento 2 Beta
Live Demo

Crafts

Crafts is a free stunning theme designed for Magento 2, which supports the latest version of the platform. Nowadays, the key feature of modern Magento themes is responsive design, and Crafts is not the exception. This e-commerce Magento template ships with responsive web design. In addition, it offers off-canvas menu and three bonus theme skins.

Themeforest

Themeforest[2] already offers a lot of Magento 2 themes. For instance, these: Porto[3] and Everything Store Magento 2[4]. More themes are reviewed here: ThemeForest Templates[5]

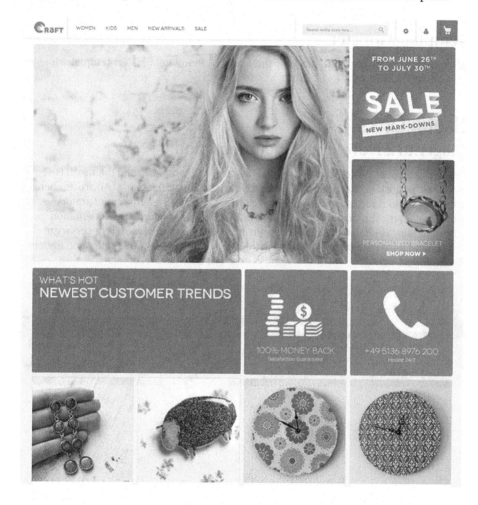

---

[2]http://themeforest.net/tags/magento2
[3]http://themeforest.net/item/porto-ultimate-responsive-magento-theme/9725864?s_phrase&s_rank=3
[4]http://themeforest.net/item/everything-store-magento-2-magento-19-multipurpose-responsive/12243332?s_phrase&s_rank=1
[5]https://firebearstudio.com/blog/tag/themeforest

Download Crafts 2.0
Crafts Installation Guide
Crafts on GitHub
Live Demo

TemplateMonster

Alternatively, check premium magento themes from TemplateMonster: TemplateMonster Magento 2 Themes[6]

Useful Links
Magento 2 Developer Documentation

Before starting any customizations related to Magento 2 templates and themes, it is extremely important to examine Magento 2 Developer Documentation. All articles here are divided into three categories: Get Started with Magento, System Administrators, and Developers. Although the information introduced in Developer Documentation covers all aspects related to such a Magento 2 component as themes, it is necessary to understand the whole platform before diving deep into Magento 2 templates and themes development.

---

[6]https://firebearstudio.com/blog/tag/TemplateMonster

Front-end Architecture of Magento 2

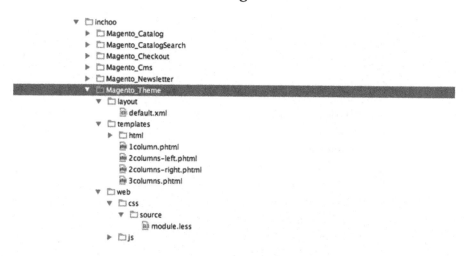

The core difference between Magento 2 and previous versions is that the front end is now updated with HTML5, CSS3, jQuery, and other newer technologies. The overall layout manipulation also differs a lot. The same is true about file structure and Magento UI library, which is now based on LESS preprocessor. The last one includes a built-in compiler.

All nuances of Magento 2 front-end architecture are described at Inchoo. The post consists of three parts. The first one is dedicated to theme workflow changes, the second part describes updates and improvements of layout, and the last one is about the new Magento UI library.

Magento 2: Serving Frontend Files

Magento 2: Serving Frontend Files. This article by Alan Storm will help you understand the way new technologies are integrated into the Magento 2 system by introducing you to such topics as Serving CSS and Javascript Files, Magento 2 Root Folder, Magento 2 Modes, Serving a Frontend Asset File, Magento 2 Static Asset Serving, etc. The information provided by Alan is vital for your further work with Magento 2 templates and themes.

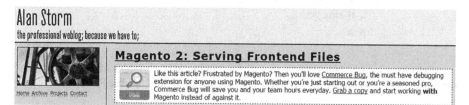

Magento 2 Theme Structure by DCKAP

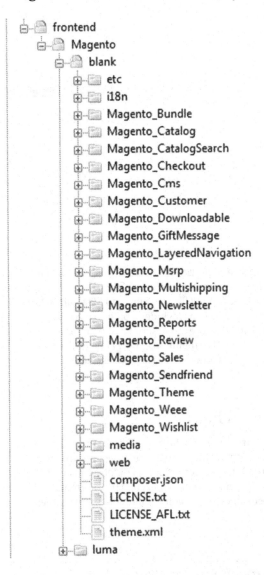

Before exploring Magento 2 themes and templates, it is extremely important to learn their structure. This topic is described in detail here: Magento 2 Theme Structure[7].

[7]http://devdocs.magento.com/guides/v2.0/frontend-dev-guide/themes/theme-structure.html

Magento 2 Theming by Shero

shero your ecommerce partner for success   Home   Our Work

Magento 2
Theming

In the Magento 2 Theming article on Shero, you can find such important things as updated PHP, CSS, and HTML requirements introduced in Magento 2; front-end development features, including CSS preprocessor, blank theme, UI library, and visual design editor; as well as key layout improvements. All these nuances are described here: Magento 2 Theming.

Core Principles for Theming in Magento 2

If you are looking for courses on Magento 2 Theming, then get ready to spend $375. For this money, you will get all the development skills necessary to implement and customize templates and themes on the popular e-commerce platforms. You can pay for the course here: Core Principles for Theming in Magento 2.

How to create a Magento 2 theme

This useful topic is covered by two sources: devdocs.magento[8] and Magestore[9]. The official documentation includes six steps. It starts with creation of a theme folder. The second step is about theme declaration. Then the post shows how to configure images in Magento 2. The fourth step teaches how to add folders for static files. The next one is about a logo for your theme. The last step teaches how to create a theme preview.

In its turn, post on Inchoo will help you understand more about Magento 2 theme and template structure. The author divides his tutorial into two parts. The first one is about primary elements in Theme package. The second part reveals the secrets of its customization in Magento 2.

Magento 2 Templates and RequireJS

RequireJS is an important tool for Magento development. Being a JavaScript[10] modular script loader, it is optimized for work within JS environments, so you can leverage all its power working with Magento 2 templates and themes. RequireJS will not only improve the quality of code, but also increase the speed of your projects. For further information, check this post: Advanced Development with RequireJS[11].

Handlebars and Magento 2 templates

With Handlebars, you can easily build semantic templates. The project is compatible with Mustache templates and in Magento 2 is used for dynamic loading of various template parts. For further information, visit its web site: Handlebars.

Grunt and Magento 2

Magento 2 templates and themes development is impossible without repetitive tasks. To streamline your routine, we recommend you to pay attention to Grunt, a JavaScript task runner. It is designed to automate such processes as compilation, linting, minification, unit testing, etc. All you need is to configure a Gruntfile. In Magento 2, Grunt simplifies the way you customize styles in a server-side compilation mode. For further information on Magento 2 themes and Grunt, follow this link: How to Use Grunt in Magento 2.[12] Additionally, there is a great article divided into two parts on Magleaks: Magento 2 Theming with Grunt / Less Part 1; Part 2.

Knockout in Magento 2 theme development

Being a stand-alone JavaScript implementation of the MVVM pattern, Knockout has a reputation of being a reliable tool which offers a clear separation between view components, domain data, and data to be displayed. Since Knockout relies on a clearly

---

[8]http://devdocs.magento.com/guides/v2.1/frontend-dev-guide/themes/theme-create.html
[9]http://blog.magestore.com/how-to-create-custom-theme-on-magento-2-part-1/
[10]https://firebearstudio.com/blog/magento-2-javascript.html
[11]https://firebearstudio.com/blog/advanced-development-with-requirejs-magento-2-tutorial.html
[12]https://firebearstudio.com/blog/magento-2-grunt.html

defined code layer, as a developer you get the ability to manage relationships between all available view components. For further information on Magento 2 theme development with Knockout, check the following links:

- The official web site

- Knockout on GitHub

- Magento 2 UI knockoutjs by Ibnab

- Knockout.js in Magento 2

- Using UI components' client-side

- Presentation Layer

CHAPTER 9

Extensions

Since Magento 2 is a new platform, there are not as many extensions available on the marketplace as in case of Magento 1.X, so we are going to explain, how to install the existing modules, and within 2016 will release the second edition of the book which will describe more Magento 2 extensions. Some modules are already available after the installation section.

How to Install Magento 2 Modules

There are several ways to install Magento 2 extensions. If you are familiar with Magento 1, they won't be complicated. Before we proceed, you can chech our blog post, How to Install Magento 2 Modules[1], for further information.

How to Install Magento 2 Extension via Composer

Now, there are only two Composer Repositories aimed at the installation of Magento 2 modules:

- the official one: Magento 2 Composer Repository

- Packagist (the official source of Composer packages) To add them to your your composer.json use the following code:

```
1    composer config repositories.magento composer
     http://packages.magento.com/
```

For packages from Packagist you don't need to add any repositories because it is the official Composer source included by default.

---

[1] https://firebearstudio.com/blog/how-to-install-magento-2-modules-extensions.html

V. Khliupko, *Magento 2 DIY*, DOI 10.1007/978-1-4842-2460-1_9

Once the repositories are added to your system, any Magento 2 extension can be installed with the aid of the following command:

```
1   composer require vendor/module
```

And then run:

```
1   composer update
```

This will install new dependencies and required Magento 2 extensions. Then run:

```
1   php bin/magento setup:upgrade
```

This command upgrades Magento 2 database.

Installing Magento 2 extension by copying code

I describe this type of installation on the example of the M2 sample module. Please note that parts like *M2demo/M2Extension* refer to *VendorName/ModuleName*. Since every Magento 2 module requires a particular directory structure (*<VendorName>/<ModuleName>*) under *<your Magento install dir>/app/code*, don't forget to replace *M2demo/M2Extension* with the particular data related to your Magento 2 extension.

Please note that you should be logged in as a user with the permission to write to your Magento web server docroot. Typically, it can be the root or web server user.

By performing the following actions, you will install your module:

1) Enter the following commands keeping their order:

```
1   cd <your Magento install dir>/app/code
2   mkdir -p M2demo/M2Extension
```

2) Go to the page of your module on Github (reference module in our case).
3) Find the Download Zip button and start your download.
4) Copy the downloaded file to your Magento server's directory: *<magento install dir>/app/code/m2demo/module- m2-extension*.
5) Run the following commands keeping their order:

```
1   unzip m2extension-master.zip
2   mv m2extension-master/* .
3   rm -rf m2extension-master
```

6) Find your <your Magento install dir>/app/etc/config.php file and open it in a text editor.

7) Add the following command under *'modules'* ⇒ *array (*:

```
1    'M2Demo_M2Extension' => 1
```

8) Save the changes and close the editor.

I'll update this Magento 2 tutorial as soon as new methods are available. If you are looking for additional information about module installation in Magento 1.x, check our post here: How to Install Magento Extensions.

Must-have Magento 2 Extensions

Although Magento 2 offers a lot of useful e-commerce features and provides top-notch performance, there is always room for improvement. And you don't need a team of specialists to enhance the default capabilities, because there are Magento 2 extensions aimed to turn your tiny e-commerce store into a robust forepost of online retail.

Although the Magento Marketplace has not been launched yet, you can already find the first Magento 2 modules on Magento connect. The web site shows available extensions and provides information on future plug-ins through the Coming Soon section. All modules are divided into several groups, which consist of different categories. To dive deep into the new Magento 2 extension marketplace, follow this link: Magento Connect.

The Magento 2 ecosystem is not as huge as the one around the first version of the platform, but it already offers some robust e-commerce solutions. Below, we are going to collect the best Magento 2 modules related to the following categories: Performance, User Experience and Front End, Import/Export, Products and Categories, SEO, Marketing and Advertising, Integrations, and Extend Magento 2 API.

Mageworx Magento 2 SEO Suite Extension[2]

---

[2]https://firebearstudio.com/blog/mageworx-magento-2-seo-suite-extension.html

This Magento 2 extension eliminates all duplicate content on your e-commerce web site, improves indexation, as well as makes it search engine-friendly. The module supports such features as: rel=canonical URLs which works on category, product, and layered navigation pages; canonical URLs for cross domain; rel="next/prev", which works on category pages; meta tags for robots; individual SEO settings for all your categories and products, etc. Besides, the Mageworx Magento 2 SEO Suite Extension offers an advanced HTML sitemap; extends settings related to XML sitemap, and optimizes the internal structure of the link. All these Magento 2 SEO improvements are available for only $149.

Improved Layered Navigation for Magento 2 by Amasty[3]

---

[3]https://firebearstudio.com/blog/amasty-improved-layered-navigation-for-magento-1-and-2.html

Chances are, your customers experience problems with navigation. Improve this drawback with the help of Improved Layered Navigation for Magento 2 by Amasty. This Magento 2 module provides your customers with the ability to search the store catalog in the most efficient and comfortable way. The extension heavily relies on filters and filter multiselect options. Besides, you get an extremely easy extension setup, while your visitors can search by product attributes and remove selected options. Such a useful set of improvements costs $139.

Follow Up Email for Magento 2 by aheadWorks[4]

Follow Up Email for Magento 2 is a smart tool that will significantly decrease your current cart abandonment rate. With this Magento 2 extension, customers' actions can become triggers which send out predefined follow-up messages to the customer. So, if someone is going to leave your store without purchasing anything, Follow Up Email for Magento 2 tries to prevent a potential customer from turning back into a visitor.

The module understands five predefined events and offers built-in templates for each follow-up case. Besides, you will get a WYSIWYG editor, which will essentially simplify your daily routine with e-mails. And for those Magento owners who need more advanced follow-up features, this tool offers the ability to create custom conditions which target highly specific events. If you have any problems with the installation or usage of Follow Up Email for Magento 2, there are reliable live support and user-friendly documentation available within the module. The tool costs $499, and this price is absolutely adequate for such a vital e-commerce features.

Simple Google Shopping for Magento 2 by Wyomind[5]

---

[4]https://firebearstudio.com/blog/aheadworks-follow-up-email-magento-2-extension-review.html

[5]https://firebearstudio.com/blog/wyomind-simple-google-shopping-for-magento-2-and-1.html

Explore Google Shopping as a new powerful source of customers with Simple Google Shopping for Magento 2 by Wyomind. With this Magento 2 extension, you will be able to export your products data to the service as easily as a piece of cake. The data feed will include all product types. Besides, you will get the ability to separate your feed into multistores, multi-VAT rates, and multicurrencies data feeds. Please note that all data feeds are generated in compliance with Google requirements. Thus, such a deep integration of Magento 2 and Google Shopping is available only via this module.

It is also necessary to mention that you will get the ability to customize all feeds according to your business requirements and products catalog, as well as rapidly discover Google categories that correspond to yours. Everything is available just for €50.

Search AutoComplete and Suggest Pro for Magento 2 by Mirasvit[6]

---

[6]https://firebearstudio.com/blog/mirasvit-search-autocomplete-suggest-pro-for-magento-2-and-1.html

Unfortunately, Magento 2 does not let your customers easily find products they are looking for, but you can improve the situation with the aid of appropriate Magento 2 extensions. In addition to the aforementioned Improved Layered Navigation module, we also recommend you install Search AutoComplete and Suggest Pro for Magento 2 by Mirasvit. Once your customer has started typing in the search box, the extension shows the drop-down list with the most suitable product names, images, and prices. In addition, you will get a 30-day free support and money back guarantee. The module costs $49.

Fooman Email Attachments[7]

In case your admins work too slowly or you spend too much time on an e-mail routine attaching various files, pay attention to Fooman Email Attachments. This free Magento 2 module provides the ability to automate the way you work with sales e-mail attachments. The extension adds Order, Shipping, Invoice, and Credit Memo PDF documents to sales e-mails. And you can easily configure everything before the system will perform all the work instead of you. As mentioned above, the module is absolutely free.

Blog for Magento 2 by AheadWorks[8]

---

[7]http://store.fooman.co.nz/extensions/magento2/magento-extension-email-attachments-m2.html
[8]https://firebearstudio.com/blog/aheadworks-blog-for-magento-2-and-1.html

Frustrated with the inability to create a professional blog on the basis of your Magento 2 web site? Your awesome posts still do not help you with your e-commerce business? The AheadWorks team knows how to solve your problem. With the aid of their Blog for Magento 2, you will get what you want: a cozy place place for your articles divided into all possible categories. The extension supports multiple stores and languages, so you can post content aimed at absolutely different target audiences. As for your customers, they will not only get a new source of stunning content, but also will be able to find posts they are looking for with ease.

Besides, this Magento 2 extension provides the ability to create links to products from your e-commerce web sites as well as other posts. Consequently, you can increase views and sales. Sitemap XML, DISQUS integration, and SEO-friendly permalinks are other features available with Blog for Magento 2.

Magento2 Delete Orders by Ibnab[9]

Magento 2 Delete Orders is another free productivity tool. This time the extension provides the ability to delete orders seamlessly instead of canceling them. As for the default Magento 2 functionality, it does not provide such an opportunity. Therefore, Ibnab's solution improves your daily work with orders significantly. You only need to select all unwanted orders in a grid and apply the mass delete option available in top actions.

---

[9]http://store.ibnab.com/magento-2-extensions/magento2-delete-orders.html

Reward Points + Referral program for Magento 2 by Mirasvit[10]

Meet the first referral extension for Magento 2: Reward Points + Referral Program for Magento 2 by Mirasvit. With this module, you will be able to reward your customers for a set of actions they perform on your e-commerce web site. For instance, if they purchase something, the extension provides them with points which can be turned into discounts. Besides, Reward Points + Referral Program supports such features as one year of free updates, 30 days money back and support, expanded user guide, etc. The extension costs $149.

---

[10]https://firebearstudio.com/blog/mirasvit-reward-points-referral-program-magento-2-and-1-review.html

Mirasvit Sphinx Search Ultimate[11]

The first reason to buy Sphinx Search Ultimate is its versatility. Mirasvit is famous as a developer of various extensions aimed at simplifying e-commerce search, and Sphinx Search Ultimate combines the company's top solutions. The extension incorporates features of such modules as Advanced Sphinx Search Pro ($99), Search AutoComplete & Suggestions ($49), and Search Spell-Correction ($49), so you get almost a $50 discount if you choose Sphinx Search Ultimate ($149).

The second reason to spend your money on this extension is its reliability. There are more than 200 reviews on the module's page and its average score on the basis of these reviews is 5/5. It seems that there are no unsatisfied customers.

The third reason to give your preference to Sphinx Search Ultimate is its incredible set of features and below we will describe the most important ones.

Imagine a situation when a new user comes to your web site for the first time. He or she probably does not know for sure how the name of a particular product is spelled. And if you don't show a hint, your new user can leave your Magento store without even placing anything in the cart. In this situation nobody increases your cart abandonment rate, but you lose a chance to turn a visitor into a buyer. But if a possible customer gets a search tip, chances that they will place an item into their cart significantly increase. The right hints help greatly to quickly find a desired product, so it is vital to provide your customers with the ability to see a drop-down with search phrases or goods from your catalog shown on the basis of what is already typed.

Another essential aspect is related to typos. In case a user made a mistake, the default search shows no results, and you lose a chance to turn a visitor into a buyer once again. Thus, all typos should be fixed by your search system to provide your visitors with what they are looking for.

Eventually, it is necessary to mention that a slow search can also distract visitors from your Magento web site. Therefore, your search solution should be lightning fast.

---

[11]https://firebearstudio.com/blog/mirasvit-sphinx-search-ultimate-for-magento-1-and-2.html

And all these characteristics are typical for the Sphinx Search Ultimate Magento extension. The search mechanism of the module is based on Sphinx, an advanced search technology that shows a highly precise result in a fraction of a second. Since your visitors get a great opportunity to find what they are looking for, you dramatically increase conversion. According to the extension's page on the Mirasvit web site, Sphinx search engine enhances conversion of visitors engaged in searching something by more than 50%. Now, let's pay close attention to key features of Sphinx Search Ultimate by Mirasvit.

Key features

- enhanced search quality

- 665 stop words

- 60,730 synonyms

- search by category names, tags, SKUs, and multiple content types (catalog products, * categories, and attributes; CMS pages; WordPress or other blog; CommerceLab; Simple Press Forum, etc.)

- typos correction

- singular/plural search

- the ability to use hyphens and slashes while searching products

- optimized for specific keywords landing pages

- fallback search

- "Out of stock" products are always in the end.

- Amazon-like search categories

- The extension relies on AJAX to show search results rapidly.

- mobile-friendly

- product data (images and prices) in the dropdown box

Besides, you can easily set a minimum number of characters to search, configure the delay in finding, as well as choose a limit for the number of results shown in the drop-down list or tips from the search box with Sphinx Search Ultimate. The extension shows high indexing speed. Its searching speed surpasses 500 queries per second against one million SKUs.

It is also necessary to mention that Sphinx supports several languages. In addition to English, it also knows Russian and Czech. And there are separate modules for Spanish, Portuguese, French, Italian, German, Romanian, Dutch, Norwegian, Swedish, Danish, Hungarian, and Finnish, so the extension is suitable for an impressive list of countries. As for spell check, it doesn't need any additional dictionaries to be installed: the content on your web site is enough. Sphinx Search Ultimate analyzes all text information available on your online store and uses it to take you customer experience to the next level.

And since Sphinx supports three working modes (MySQL- based built-in search engine; Sphinx Engine on the same server; Sphinx Engine on the external server), Mirasvit's module is suitable for online stores of all sizes.

AheadWorks Advanced Reports for Magento 2[12]

AheadWorks Advanced Reports for Magento 2 is not as robust as its predecessor, but it is already a reliable tool for Magento 2 that adds some missing features. With this module, you will get only six reports (more reports should be available soon), a report drill-down with expanded data, and stunning visual graphs for each report.

The available basic reports provide the ability to evaluate general performance of your Magento 2 web site from different perspectives. First of all, you get a complete sales overview that assembles core sales KPIs in a convenient table. Then, there is a report on product performance that breaks sales down by individual products. Other stats are gathered around categories, payment types, coupon codes, and manufacturers.

As for report drill-downs, they provide the ability to combine several reports on one interface with responsive settings and a breadcrumb trail. As a result, the minimum time is required to adjust and navigate the reports. You can break any given period by such periods as day, week, month, quarter, or year. And there is no need to return to Magento report selection for switching between reports, since there is an appropriate drop-down menu. Furthermore, you can even contact support and access the extension's documentation right from the Advanced Reports Magento 2 extension.

AheadWorks Email Marketing Pack Magento Extension[13]

---

[12]https://firebearstudio.com/blog/aheadworks-advanced-reports-for-magento-2-and-1.html
[13]https://firebearstudio.com/blog/magento-email-marketing-pack-by-aheadworks.html

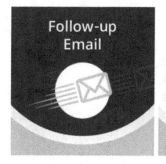  

If you are interested in improving the default e-mail marketing functionality of Magento, but do not want to spend time on comparing all available extensions, pay attention to Magento Email Marketing Pack by AheadWorks. With this module, you will not only avoid the hell of choosing among multiple available options but also save $160. Specialists from AheadWorks have developed 3 useful tools that will revamp the way you run your e-mail marketing campaigns and you can get them as a single suite.

Email Marketing Pack offers a combination of the following modules:

- Follow Up Email[14] —$199

- Market Segmentation Suite[15] —$199

- Advanced Newsletter[16] —$139

Unlike other Magento companies, AheadWorks has implemented the following mechanism: you have to add all three modules to your cart to purchase them with the $160 discount. You still have to install the modules separately, but it doesn't influence their excellent e-mail marketing capabilities. They make a great marketing combo, so you can easily reach different customer groups with surgical accuracy.

---

[14]https://firebearstudio.com/blog/aheadworks-follow-up-email-magento-2-extension-review.html
[15]http://ecommerce.aheadworks.com/magento-extensions/market-segmentation-suite.html?cmid=SVhUd01JTTdDZ1k9&afid=NC91QSs4N0FyeDg9&ats=VHQ3cWdaYWNzbU09
[16]http://ecommerce.aheadworks.com/magento-extensions/advanced-newsletter.html?cmid=SVhUd01JTTdDZ1k9&afid=NC91QSs4N0FyeDg9&ats=VHQ3cWdaYWNzbU09

M2 Extension Pack by AheadWorks[17]

We already have a lot of different digests related to various Magento 2 extensions, but if a wide variety of Magento 2 modules scares you, purchase a starter pack offered by a reliable Magento developer. In the near future, we are going to overview such sets produced by the most popular Magento companies, and today we will introduce you to M2 Extension Pack by AheadWorks.

So what is M2 Extension Pack? It's a set of Magento 2 extensions by AheadWorks launched before March 31st, 2016. You pay only once and get an unlimited access to all these modules. Sounds intriguing, isn't it?

Let's describe the content of the Magento 2 starter pack. The company promises to launch 12 extensions before March 31st, covering the core e-commerce functionality from scratch. AheadWorks also states that it is the best value-for-the-money offer available on the Magento 2 market. Furthermore, if you are a Magento 1 owner, you can get a 30% discount for our Magento 1 extensions. You only need a M2PACK coupon code.

But what exactly is in the pack? AheadWorks offers a unique opportunity for start-up stores to get up to speed with core functionality extensions from such areas as: Sales and Marketing; Administration; Content Management; and User Experience. This is the full list of Magento 2 modules available with M2 Extension Pack:

- Automatic Related Products

- Follow Up Email

- Gift Card

- Advanced Reports

- RMA

- Product Questions

- Blog

---

[17]https://firebearstudio.com/blog/m2-extension-pack-magento-2-starter-pack-by-aheadworks.html

- Custom Static Blocks

- Store Locator

- Layered Navigation

- AJAX Cart Pro

- Social Login

Now, we will pay much closer attention to each AheadWorks Magento 2 extension from M2 Extension Pack.

Automatic Related Products[18]

Automatic Related Products for Magento 2 provides the ability to manage blocks of related product across your Magento 2 web site. The extension essentially simplifies the way you create and customize them due to the following features:

- First of all, it provides flexible conditions for defining your related products.

- Then, you get various options that help you with the layout customization of the block.

- And of course you can choose any position for your blocks on a product page or in a shopping cart.

---

[18]https://firebearstudio.com/blog/aheadworks-automatic-related-products-magento-2-review.html

That's how the Automatic Related Products Magento 2 extension works. Follow Up Email[19]

Follow Up Email is another robust option available with M2 Extension Pack.This Magento 2 extension automatically sends out follow-up messages based on customer activity. You get 5 predefined events that trigger an e-mail as well as the ability to create custom conditions for specific events. Besides, the Follow Up Email Magento 2 extension offers:

- predefined e-mail templates for each follow-up case;

- user-friendly WYSIWYG editor.

Follow Up Email is one of the most reliable tools designed to reduce your cart abandonment rate. Besides, it will help you communicate with your customers and make them more loyal due to such follow-up events as birthday, new registration, or long period of inactivity.

Gift Card[20]

---

[19]https://firebearstudio.com/blog/aheadworks-follow-up-email-magento-2-extension-review.html
[20]https://firebearstudio.com/blog/aheadworks-gift-card-magento-2-review.html

If you've never used gift cards in your e-commerce business then it's time to try, because AheadWorks offers a tool that creates a perfect gift card made in compliance with your business standards. You can easily add both physical and virtual gift cards to the catalog. The design of the card is fully customizable. Furthermore, you can implement an individual approach to all your customers, since they get the ability to write personal messages upon every purchase. Other notable features are:

- You can delivere cards from the Magento 2 back end.

- All issued cards and their usage are tracked from the back end.

Advanced Reports[21]

Get the Advanced Reports Magento 2 extensions and dive deep into detailed statistics related to your e-commerce business. The analytical tool by AheadWorks not only provides a clear view of various performance areas but also allows you to run a quick evaluation of your online storefront.

With the extensions, you get six reports describing sales over time. Each report offers extra data with each click and visual graphs illustrate trends for each report. Thus, Advanced Reports offers a great opportunity to explore your Magento 2 web site.

---

[21]https://firebearstudio.com/blog/aheadworks-advanced-reports-for-magento-2-and-1.html

RMA[22]

By installing this Magento 2 extension, you take care of all RMA aspects possible in your online business. First of all, you get an intuitive submission form for RMA request creation. Furthermore, your customers do not need to be logged in, because guest requests are possible from an appropriate store page.

Another important aspect is related to robust back-end management available due to step-by-step RMA processing. Besides, you get two-way notifications for status changes with RMA by AheadWorks. As for extension settings aimed at adjusting various workflow elements, they are also available.

Product Questions[23]

With this module, you will be closer to your customers, since the Product Questions Magento 2 extension adds a communication area for each product page. As a result, your customers can leave inquiries as well as share information about your products.

---

[22]https://firebearstudio.com/blog/aheadworks-rma-for-magento-2-and-1.html
[23]https://firebearstudio.com/blog/aheadworks-product-questions-magento-2-extension-review.html

All answers can be provided by both customers or administrators. And nobody will lose an answer, since there is a reliable notification system. Besides, there is a rating system that sorts information by relevance.

Blog[24]

Every Magento web site needs a blog. You can promote your content there, post useful tutorials, or tell your customers something interesting, making them more loyal. Unfortunately, the default platform does not have this tool out-of-the-box, but you can easily solve this problem with the Blog Magento 2 extension by AheadWorks.

With the module, you will get a content editor with all essential writing/design tools; SEO improvements; categories, and sidebar blocks, as well as DISQUS integration for fast comment management. Also check FishPig WordPress integration for Magento 2[25].

Custom Static Blocks[26]

---

[24]https://firebearstudio.com/blog/aheadworks-blog-for-magento-2-and-1.html
[25]https://fishpig.co.uk/magento-2/wordpress-integration/
[26]https://firebearstudio.com/blog/aheadworks-custom-static-blocks-magento-2-extension-review.html

Content management on Magento has never been so easy! Install the Custom Static Blocks, and you will be able to manage customizable blocks of content within your e-commerce web site. Available content types range from from banners to widgets and videos.

Another important feature represented with this extension is the ability to display different blocks to different customer groups. Scheduling options are also available with the extension.

Store Locator[27]

This Magento 2 extension is a very simple but vital solution if you have a brick-and-mortar store. The module provides customers with the ability to find nearby locations of your offline shop. It is integrated with Google Maps, appropriate store information is listed for each individual location, and your clients can search by address or run radius search.

Besides, there is an opportunity to use any custom image as a store photo. The same is true about map markers.

Layered Navigation[28]

[27]https://firebearstudio.com/blog/aheadworks-store-locator-for-magento-2-and-1.html
[28]https://firebearstudio.com/blog/aheadworks-layered-navigation-magento-2-extension-review.html

Make the navigation of your web site user-friendly and you will increase sales. You only need a reliable module, and AheadWorks has such a tool. With the company's Layered Navigation, you add an enhancement that turns native layered navigation of Magento 2 into a more convenient system.

The extension adds three new filter options, provides the ability to select multiple attributes, and eliminates intermediary page reloads. Unlike in the native Magento 2 solution, your customers can select several attributes of a single filter simultaneously. It is also necessary to mention that the navigation process isn't interrupted by reloads each time our customer selects a new attribute.

Moreover, the Layered Navigation Magento 2 extension shows how many items match each selection.

AJAX Cart Pro[29]

Wish to have a modern cart? Then you should implement the AJAX technology in this area of your Magento 2 web site. And one of the easiest ways to do so is offered by AheadWorks. You only need to install the AJAX Cart Pro Magento 2 extension, and the desired features will be available to your customers.

Features available with this module include:

- add-to-cart popup window that provides the ability to select product options without visiting a product page;

- various product information in the pop-up;

- full mobile support;

- support for all product types available in Magento 2.

---

[29]https://firebearstudio.com/blog/aheadworks-ajax-cart-pro-for-magento-2-and-1.html

Social Login[30]

Social Login is another simple but quite useful extension for Magento 2. It provides a registration form that allows customers to log in via their social network accounts. They can use Facebook, Twitter, LinkedIn, or Google. More options will be available soon. Besides, the Social Login Magento 2 extension by AheadWorks provides the ability to link an existing store account to a social network profile. As for social login buttons, they are available at both checkout and customer login.

uMarketplace Suite Multi-Vendor Marketplace for Magento 2[31]

You might have heard about uMarketplace Suite Multi-Vendor Marketplace for 1.X. This extension is quite expensive ($1,650), but it does its work seamlessly, transforming your store into a feature-rich e-commerce shopping mall. The same functionality is available for Magento 2, so get ready for multiple independent vendors selling their products via your store with a centralized product catalog and uniquely themed microsites.

With the aid of this Magento 2 multivendor marketplace extension, you provide vendors with the ability to add and edit products and images, assign attribute values and applicable categories, manage shipments, shipping options, and inventory, update account data, as well as communicate with their customers and your store admins. Besides, all your vendors can reject or confirm orders, view order history, enter shipment tracking, as well as create shipping labels and packing slips.

Besides, uMarketplace Suite is absolutely friendly to drop shipping: the extension offers all the tools required for configuring and automating the workflow. That's because uMarketplace Suite Multi-Vendor Marketplace for Magento 2 is based on the uDropShip extension, a module that powers thousands of Magento stores.

---

[30]https://firebearstudio.com/blog/aheadworks-social-login-for-magento-2-and-1.html
[31]https://secure.unirgy.com/products/umarketplace/magento-multi-vendor-marketplace

Key features of this multi vendor marketplace solution include:

- product catalog and order management revamped with multi vendor functionality in mind;

- universal checkout system for each order adopted for products from various vendors with different shipping origins;

- a bunch of automated processes. For instance, purchase orders are generated on the basis of customer sales order;

- intuitive vendor interface for convenient product and order management;

- full control over product approval with the ability to approve items related to certain vendors automatically;

- a bunch of commission rates based on various conditions;

- vendor financial statements that can be created manually or automatically;

- Vendor Vacation Mode, when vendors can suspend their activity;

- different checkout methods;

- robust notification system for both vendors and their customers;

- custom API integration for vendors;

- custom shipping costs for each vendor and region-based shipping rates.

More Magento 2 extensions for building a multivendor marketplace, are gathered here: Magento 2 Multi Vendor Marketplace[32].

Another extremely important tool is Improved Import by our team. It provides a possibility to import your CSV files with product data and images to Magento 2 from a remote FTP server, Dropbox or a direct URL of a source CSV file. Besides, the module improves the default functionality with dedicated category import from csv files, on-the-fly import of product attribute values, cron job import and more. Firebear Improved Import is a great time-saver that adds advanced functionality to Magento 2.

With Improved Import, you will get the following features:

- regular product stock updates with any frequency: every minute or once a month

- product info and stock sync with external CRM/ERP/PIM or any other system. It is only necessary to set up csv file data and create Cron job import in Magento 2 admin.

- export product, category and customer data to a remote FTP server for further usage by external CRM / ERP / PIM systems

---

[32]https://firebearstudio.com/blog/magento-2-multi-vendor-marketplace.html

- full circle Magento 2 and Dropbox integration. Streamline the world's most popular cloud storage and file collaboration tool in your Magento 2 routine! Import and export products, categories, and customers to Dropbox and get a new level of team collaboration. By sharing import and export folders on Dropbox, you will simplify Magento inventory management and make it more affordable than ever before. In a combination with import cron jobs, you can edit your csv file on your Dropbox folder and get all data updated in a Magento 2 database in minutes!

Download the extension here: Improved Import for Magento 2[33]. For further information, check this review: Improved Import Magento 2 Extension Manual[34].

Additionally, you can check the following companies, because they always release reliable extensions:

- Fooman[35]

- Ebizmarts[36]

- Amasty[37]

- AheadWorks[38]

- Mirasvit[39]

- Mageworx[40]

- Ibnab[41]

- Wyomind[42]

And don't forget about Magento Connect[43]. Some new Magento 2 extensions are already available there. As for the Magento Marketplace, it is described here[44].

Being a robust e-commerce web site built upon the Magento platform, Magento Marketplace offers integrated payments via credit cards and PayPal. It hosts both free and paid modules, services, and themes. The launch of Magento Marketplace is planned for 2016. It will be a much more secure and robust e-commerce option than Magento Connect, but unfortunately with a 70/30 revenue share split.

---

[33]https://firebearstudio.com/the-improved-import.html
[34]https://firebearstudio.com/blog/improved-import-magento-2-extension-manual.html
[35]http://store.fooman.co.nz/extensions/magento2
[36]https://store.ebizmarts.com/magento-2-extensions
[37]https://firebearstudio.com/blog/tag/Amasty
[38]https://firebearstudio.com/blog/tag/AheadWorks
[39]https://firebearstudio.com/blog/tag/Mirasvit
[40]https://firebearstudio.com/blog/tag/Mageworx
[41]http://store.ibnab.com/magento-2-extensions.html
[42]https://firebearstudio.com/blog/tag/Wyomind
[43]https://www.magentocommerce.com/magento-connect/magento-2
[44]https://firebearstudio.com/blog/magento-connect-2-0-facts-thoughts-and-expectations.html

Alternatively, you can search for free modules on GitHub, or check Firebear's posts: The Best Magento 2 Extensions[45], Must Have Magento 2 Extensions For Advanced E-commerce Experience[46], and Magento 2 Extensions Reviewed On Firebear[47].

---

[45]https://firebearstudio.com/blog/the-best-magento-2-extensions.html
[46]https://firebearstudio.com/blog/magento-2-extensions-for-advanced-ecommerce.html
[47]https://firebearstudio.com/blog/magento-2-extensions-reviewed-on-firebear.html

CHAPTER 10

■ ■ ■

SEO

Among all e-commerce platform, Magento is the most powerful in terms of SEO. It provides the ability to optimize site URLs, page titles, meta and ALT tags, headings, and other web site elements out-of-the-box. Additionally, there is an impressive selection of various third party Magento modules designed to improve the default SEO capabilities. As for Magento 2, it provides even better SEO options. The new version of the popular e-commerce platform has been fully revamped, therefore we'd like to introduce you to Magento 2 SEO[1].

Magento 2 SEO Features

- Product Page: metadata, canonical tag, product URLs

- Category Page: meta tags, SEO-friendly category URL key

- Pagination: canonical tag

---

[1]https://firebearstudio.com/blog/magento-2-seo.html

V. Khliupko, *Magento 2 DIY*, DOI 10.1007/978-1-4842-2460-1_10

- Layered Navigation: canonical tag

- XML Sitemap: priority and frequency for each page type, robots. txt file integration

- Rich Snippets are the most anticipated Magento 2 SEO feature.

- Robots.txt is now editable from the Admin panel.

- Schema.org is added to a default Magento 2 Template.

- Product Image Labels is another Magento 2 SEO feature.

- Related products, Upsells, and Cross-sells are also optimized in Magento 2.

- Universal Google Analytics, E-commerce Tracking, and AdWords Conversion are available out-of- the-box.

- Google Tag Manager is a unique feature of Magento 2 Enterprise Edition.

Below, we describe all the aforementioned features.

Product Page Optimization

Since Magento 1.X offered quite robust product page optimization, only a few things have been added in Magento 2. Every product page still has the same meta tag settings with the ability to set up such standard tags as: meta title, description, and keywords. As a Magento administrator, you can do this per each Store View; the same is true about the Product URL Key.

Mask for SKU	{{name}}

Use {{name}} as Product Name placeholder

Mask for Meta Title	{{name}}

Use {{name}} as Product Name placeholder

Mask for Meta Keywords	{{name}}

Use {{name}} as Product Name or {{sku}} as Product SKU placeholders

Mask for Meta Description	{{name}} {{description}}

Use {{name}} and {{description}} as Product Name and Product Description placeholders

As for new Magento 2 SEO features related to product page optimization, there is Product Fields Auto-Generation. The new option can be utilized to form the product meta tags with the aid of available product attributes and predefined templates. You can find the Auto-Generation feature under Stores/- Configuration/Catalog.

The way you set up a Canonical Link meta tag for your products in Magento 2 is the same as in 1.X. For instance, `http://yourstore.com/samsung-2511.html?referal=13457` is referred to as `http://yourstore.com/samsung-2511.html`. You can change your canonical link options under Stores/Configuration/Catalog/Search Engine Optimization. To create SEO-friendly URLs in Magento 2, you can include their categories path as in Magento 1 under the same options.

Category Page Optimization

Magento 2 SEO features related to category page optimization include the same standard meta tags as title, meta description, and meta keywords, and you can set them up per each Store View. The same is true about a category URL key. But unlike 1.X, Magento 2 does not include available filter options, so the category page URL always remains the same.

Page Title	
Meta Keywords	
Meta Description	

Pagination Optimization

Pagination in Magento 2 is optimized with a canonical tag. As a result, the URL points to the category itself. For example, a URL such as *http://yourstore.com/products.html?p=3* points to *http://yourstore.com/products.html*.

Layered Navigation Optimization

Layered navigation optimization in Magento 2 is also based on a canonical tag. As a result, URLs of layered navigation pages point to their categories, so selected attributes are not added to meta tags. Thus, *http://www.yourstore.com/t-shirts/mens-t-shirts.html?color=black&manufacturer=nike&price=10-50* refers to *http://www.yourstore.com/t-shirts/mens-t-shirts.html*.

XML Sitemap

An XML sitemap now has a bunch of improvements. Thus, you can specify the priority and frequency for product, category, CMS, and other pages separately. Furthermore, the new Magento 2 SEO functionality provides the ability to add your XML sitemap to a robots.txt file automatically. Besides, the new version of the platform provides the ability to add images, use the Sitemap Index, and define parameters necessary for splitting items between various XML files.

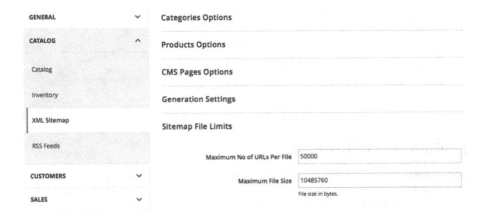

Rich Snippets

The ability to add rich snippets is the most anticipated Magento 2 SEO feature. With its help, you can easily show structured markup data from your e-commerce web site within Google results. The new improvement helps to improve both SEO and CTR. And it is enabled by default.

Amazon.com: Bose® **QuietComfort®** 15 Acoustic Noise Cancelling ...
www.amazon.com › ... › Audio & Video Accessories › Headphones
★★★★★ Rating: 4.4 - 312 reviews - $299.00 - In stock
QuietComfort 15 headphones feature exclusive Bose advancements in noise reduction
technology. You hear less noise and more of your music and ...

[PDF] **QUIETCOMFORT®** 15 - Bose   **Rich Snippets**
www.bose.no/.../owners-guide_QuietComfort_15_headphones...
File Format: PDF/Adobe Acrobat - Quick View
QUIETCOMFORT® 15. ACOUSTIC NOISE CANCELLING® HEADPHONES. Q. UIE.
TC. OM. FORT. ®. 15. A. CO. US. T. IC. N. OIS. E. C. AN. CE. LL. ING. ®. H. E ...

Bose **QuietComfort** 15 Acoustic Noise Cancelling Headphones ...
www.bestbuy.com/...**QuietComfort**%26%23174%3B-15.../945...
★★★★★ Rating: 5 - Review by from Cuyahoga Falls, OH on ... - Apr 1,
2013 - $299.99 - In stock
BOSE **QuietComfort** 15 Acoustic Noise Cancelling Headphones: Noise-canceling
design; rare earth magnet; TriPort® acoustic headphone structure; 5-1/2' cord ...

Robots.txt

Another important Magento 2 SEO feature is the ability to edit a robots.txt file in the admin panel under Stores/General/Design.

Alternatively, you can utilize our optimised robots.txt for Magento 2 Community Edition and Magento 2 Enterprise Edition. Grab the extension for free from GitHub: magento2robotstxt.

Design	Search Engine Robots		
Contacts			
Reports	Default Robots	INDEX, FOLLOW ▼	[STORE VIEW]
		This will be included before head closing tag in page HTML.	
Content Management	Edit custom instruction of robots.txt File		[STORE VIEW]
CATALOG ⌄			
CUSTOMERS ⌄	Reset to Defaults	Reset to Default	
SALES ⌄		This action will delete your custom instructions and reset robots.txt file to system's default settings.	

Schema.org Integration

Schema.org is now added to a default Magento 2 template. Its vocabulary is used for marking up web site content with metadata about itself. This improvement helps search engines get a better understanding of your Magento web site.

Product Image Labels

Another crucial Magento 2 SEO feature is the ability to use product labels. Now, you can not only draw your customers' attention but also improve SEO by applying labels to product images. Such options are available in 1.X, but only via third-party extensions.

Related products, Upsells, and Cross-sells

These are three types of product relations in Magento. Upsell, for example, is a product that you'd like your visitor to purchase instead the one that is already chosen, so it appears in the shopping cart. Such a product is always pricey and has better quality. Related products appear on the product page and can be purchased in addition to the product that the customer is viewing. As for Cross-sells, they appear on product pages and in the cart being products related to an impulse buy. All three types are optimized for better SEO in Magento 2.

Universal Google Analytics, E-commerce Tracking, and AdWords Conversion

Universal Analytics adds a set of options aimed at collecting and organizing data for a better understanding of your customers' behaviour and consequently improving current SEO. But before Google Analytics can report e-commerce activity for your Magento store, it is necessary to enable e-commerce tracking for your web site, which is significantly simplified in case of Magento 2. As for conversion tracking, it can help you find out how effectively your keywords engage your customers to perform certain actions. Therefore, it is another important SEO improvement introduced in Magento 2. All three features are available by default, which is a great SEO improvement introduced in Magento 2.

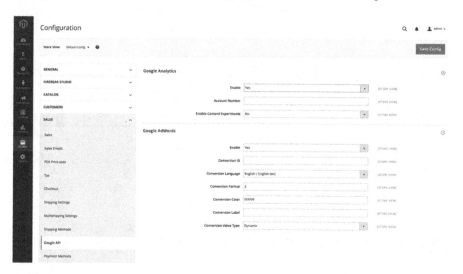

Google Tag Manager

Google Tag Manager provides the ability to create and update tags for your Magento web site any time you want, so you get better SEO opportunities. Please note that this Magento 2 feature is available only for Enterprise Edition merchants.

SEO configuration

It is also necessary to mention that all SEO settings available in 1.X are still on their usual places under Stores/Configuration/Catalog/SEO.

Conclusion

The default SEO capabilities of the platform have been essentially improved in Magento 2, so it is more powerful than its predecessor. If the default SEO options are not enough for satisfying your business needs, then you can use various third-party solutions.

Please note that lots of core SEO improvements are still in progress, so you can check them on GitHub.

To improve your Magento 2 SEO even more, we recommend you choose one of the following extensions: Mageworx Magento 2 SEO Suite[2], Amasty SEO Toolkit[3], or Mirasvit Advanced SEO Suite[4]. These modules are all-in-one solutions designed to improve the search engine-friendliness of all platform areas.

CHAPTER 11

Performance

Good performance is a key aspect of a successful e-commerce project. It is not only important as a vital ranking factor, but is highly appreciated by customers. Thus, a fast online store often has a higher conversion rate than a slower one. As a result, it turns more visitors into buyers and helps to increase sales. Now, when the importance of Magento 2 performance is obvious, it's time to shed light on how to increase it in the case of the platform[1].

We already have a detailed guide to Magento 1.X productivity, but the second version of the platform differs a lot and requires another approach to performance improvements. Magento 2 is faster, less resource-hungry, and better optimized for high loads than 1.X. Besides, it offers a lot of new performance features out-of-the-box. For instance, you get native support for Varnish, Redis, and Nginx as well as full page caching in Magento 2. As for the first version of the e-commerce platform, all these features were only available through customizations and extensions.

Although Magento 2 provides better opportunities related to performance, there is still a lot of work to be done before your e-commerce store will be as fast as the platform allows. You can check the appropriate article on Firebear, The Magento 2 Performance Guide[2], but now we will start with Nginx.

---

[1]https://firebearstudio.com/blog/magento-2.html
[2]https://firebearstudio.com/blog/the-magento-2-performance-guide-out-of-the-box-features-extensions-tips.html

Full Nginx Support

Nginx has been developed with three core principles in mind: high performance, high concurrency, and low usage of memory. Thus, it significantly increases the speed of every web site. To handle requests, Nginx utilizes an event-driven asynchronous approach, while the default Magento 1.X is based on a process-oriented approach with the Event MPM as the asynchronous processing model. Due to event-driven architecture, Nginx shows more predictable performance even under higher loads.

As mentioned above, Magento 2 offers a native support for this solution, so it can be easily installed on top of the platform. To find out how to perform this procedure, check this Magento 2 Nginx Configuration[3] guide. Besides, Magento 2 has a recommended Nginx configuration in the root folder. You can also check it on GitHub here.

Magento 2 and Redis

Redis is an advanced key-value cache which provides top notch performance and offers such features as value incrementation in a hash; pushing an element to a list; appending to a string; getting a sorted set of members with the highest ranking; and set intersection, union and difference computing.

It incorporates several use cases for in-memory datasets, which are the reason for high performance results. Thus, you can either persist it by dumping the dataset to disk or append each command to a log. Moreover, if you need a feature-rich, in-memory cache, the persistence can be disabled.

Additionally, Redis incorporates non-blocking synchronization and auto-reconnection with resynchronization partial on net split. All these features make it a lightning-fast solution for every e-commerce web site, especially for a Magento store.

If you don't know how to install and use Redis with the second version of the popular e-commerce platform, check this Magento 2 guide: Magento 2 Redis Configuration[4].

Different Cache Types

Magento works with the following types of cache:

- Configuration cache appears when Magento gathers configuration from modules. It also includes store-specific settings from database and the file system.

- Layout cache includes compiled page layouts.

- Block HTML output cache consists of HTML page fragments per each block.

- Collections data cache gathers database queries.

---

[3]https://firebearstudio.com/blog/magento-2-nginx-configuration.html
[4]https://firebearstudio.com/blog/magento-2-redis-configuration.html

- DDL cache is designed to work with database schema.

- Entity attribute value cache includes Metadata related to EAV attributes: store labels, attribute rendering, search settings, etc.

- Page cache gathers data about generated HTML pages.

- Translations cache is related to merged translations from modules.

- Integration configuration cache is aimed at compiled integrations.

- Integration API configuration cache consists of compiled integration APIs.

- Web services configuration cache is the cache of a web API structure.

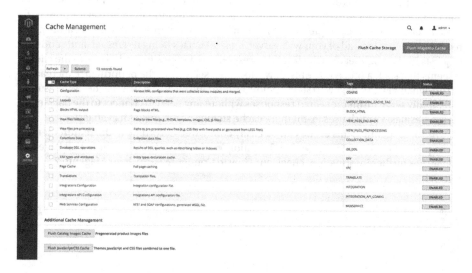

You can find appropriate configurations under System ➤ Cache Management. For further information, check our Magento 2 Cache Management[5] guide.

Full Page Cache (FPC)

Full page caching is so powerful due to the ability to store the full page output in a cache. As a result, subsequent page loads do not require much server load. Thus, full page caching is mandatory for high- traffic web sites, as it keeps server load as low as possible and helps to avoid downtime even when traffic is really high. In addition, by using full page caching, you will increase the speed of your e-commerce web site, since all the server needs will be reduced to fetching and rendering pages from the cache.

---

[5]https://firebearstudio.com/blog/magento-2-cache-management.html

If necessary, Magento can clean up this cache automatically, but you can still put any data in any segment of the cache manually. Please note that it is necessary to clean or flush FPC after modifying any code level that affects HTML output. Always keep this cache enabled, since it significantly improves the performance of Magento 2.

Varnish Cache

Varnish cache is an HTTP accelerator for heavily consumed APIs and content-heavy dynamic web sites. Magento 2 supports this cache out of the box, you can easily configure it for your e-commerce project to increase the default performance.

Every web server receives HTTP requests, but does not return HTTP responses immediately. Therefore, a long sequence of steps is required for each request. Multiplied by thousands of requests, these steps lead to server overloads, heavy resource consumption, and a significant performance decrease. Unfortunately, the server does not remember even repeated requests, but you can fix this problem with the aid of Varnish. It receives requests instead of your web server, looks at what's being requested, and sends requests to your web server, which sends a response to Varnish to pass it back to the client. It seems that such a procedure only slows down the server, but the performance increase occurs when Varnish begins to store responses from the back end in its cache. As a result, it can rapidly serve further repeated responses without any need to connect to the back-end server. Besides, Varnish uses in-memory cache storage which makes it even faster.

As for Magento 2, this cache can be easily configured according to the requirements of the platform under STORES ➤ Configuration ➤ ADVANCED ➤ System ➤ Full Page Cache. For further information, check our How to Configure Varnish for Magento 2 tutorial.

CSS Preprocessing

Although CSS has a very powerful syntax, it can easily grow to enormous sizes when working on non-trivial projects. Luckily, we can easily fix this problem with the help of CSS preprocessors: SASS and LESS. Both allow additional leverage over CSS by offering enhanced syntax, but for the Magento 2 development we will focus on LESS. It's core features are:

- nested syntax;

- ability to define variables and mixins;

- operational and mathematical functions;

- multiple files joining.

If you are not familiar with this CSS preprocessor, pay attention to the following documentation:

- Magento 2 CSS preprocessing

- Create symlinks to LESS files

CSS and JS minification

In Magento 2, CSS and JS minification procedures are almost the same as in the case of 1.X. By combining, compressing, and caching Javascript[6] and CSS files, you can improve the performance of your Magento 2 web site. Thus, it's only a matter of time when appropriate tools will be available. Besides, you can perform everything manually:

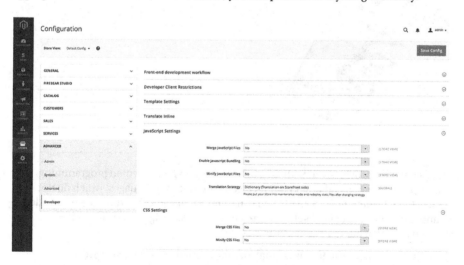

---

[6]https://firebearstudio.com/blog/magento-2-javascript.html

Catalog images caching

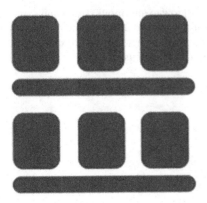

Magento pre-generates cropped product images in different sizes to reduce processing on every page load. Thumbnails are generated during the first image load and can be easily removed.

Code Generation

Code generation provides you with the ability to bring aspect-oriented programming, generic programming, and other complicated techniques to languages, which do not support them by default. As a result, you can improve Magento 2 performance and add unique features to the default setup. There are two ways to trigger code generation in Magento 2. First of all, you can perform it on the fly:

- Use a meaningful name that follows a certain pattern to declare a class.

- Now, the system should autoload the class. If it can not find it, the class will be generated.

Unfortunately, this approach slows down the system, so we recommend you utilize the command line. By using the following command, you will force the system to inspect the code and generate all necessary classes.

```
1   magento setup:di:compile
```

This approach speeds up the system, so it is useful for production.

With the aid of both approaches, you will get generated classes in the *MAGENTO_ ROOT/var/generation* directory.

For further information check this article: Introduction to code generation in Magento 2.

RequireJS for Improved JS Performance

There is the official documentation related to the configuration of JavaScript resources, but we are going to focus our attention on RequireJS. Being a JavaScript modular script loader, this tool is optimized for both JS environments and in-browser use; therefore, it is best suited for Magento 2. RequireJS is used to improve the quality of code and the speed of apps. Since JavaScript does not provide any ways for specifying code required to execute a file, RequireJS plays a crucial role in the improvement of JS development: it specifies dependencies between JS files and loads them into a browser. Such an improvement leads to a significant jump in performance; therefore, we recommend you check this article: Advanced Development with RequireJS + Magento 2 Tutorial[7].

Session Storage Management

Another useful performance improvement is related to session storage management. You can move it from files to the database or Redis. Use the *-session-save* option with any of the following:

- *db* will move it to the database. It is necessary to choose database storage in case of a clustered database.

- *redis* will move it the Redis back end.

- *files* should be used to store session data in the file system.

We strongly recommend you store everything in Redis, since Magento 2 fully supports it and you can prevent your store from performance degradation. In case of a large number of users, both your database and file system suffer a dramatic decrease in productivity. As a result, your Magento 2 web site slows down, leading to a terrible user experience. Thus, Redis is the only reliable option.

---

[7]https://firebearstudio.com/blog/advanced-development-with-requirejs-magento-2-tutorial.html

Out-Of-The-Box CDN Support

Since Magento 2 also provides support for CDN support, media and static content can be loaded from separate subdomains located on different servers of CDN networks. CDN options can be configured under Stores ➤ Configuration ➤ Web.

PHP 7[8]

Besides tons of new features and improvements introduced in PHP 7, we will get a language with completely new performance. It will be much faster than the latest available 5.X, and Magento 2 will fully support it. Thus, PHP 7 will change our understanding of how fast an e-commerce shop could be. For a deeper insight into PHP 7, check this post: PHP 7 - features, release date, rumors; and don't forget to examine a current problem related to PHP 7 and Magento 2: String class name issue for php7[9].

---

[8]https://firebearstudio.com/blog/tag/php-7
[9]https://firebearstudio.com/blog/php-7-features-release-date-rumors.html

Magento 2 vs Magento 1

You can compare the performance of both platforms via MageMeter, an amazing service from Inchoo. From the following picture, we can see that the latest Magento 2 beta with disabled caches already beats Magento 1 Enterprise Edition:

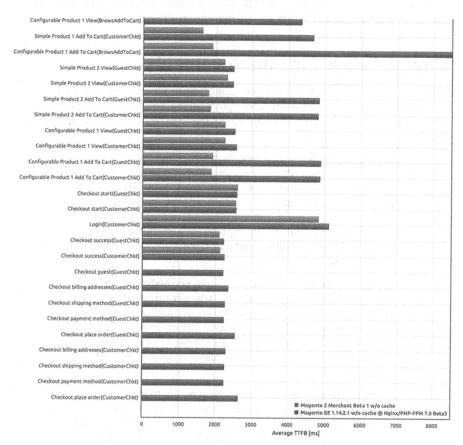

Magento 2 Extensions[10]

You can check our list of Magento 2 modules on the blog, but the platform is still too young to create a separate article related to performance extensions. We expect that all the most-wanted Magento 2 performance modules will replace their Magento 1.X ancestors. Improved Full Page cache , JS/CSS Minification , CDN services, and dozens of other tools will be available soon.

---

[10]https://firebearstudio.com/blog/the-best-magento-2-extensions.html

For instance, the second version of our Control for CloudFlare extension allows you to control the CloudFlare system directly from your Magento 2 admin. It offers better integration as well as more flexible connections between Magento 2 and CloudFlare than its first version. Thus, we anticipate that Magento 2 performance extensions will provide a better experience than their current analogs.

Besides, we recommend you check Magento 2 modules reviewed on Firebear. All tools are divided by companies: Magento 2 Extensions reviewed on Firebear[11].

General Server Side Improvements

Although the new version of Magento offers tons of improvements compared to 1.X, there are still a lot of common performance optimizations. You can find all of them in our Magento Performance Ultimate Guide. Check the links below to find the appropriate tutorials"

- OPcache is a code-caching module designed to improve that part of your Magento 2 performance which is related to PHP. It uses a shared memory for storing precompiled script bytecode. Thus, OPcache eliminates the PHP's need for loading and parsing scripts on every request. Therefore, by optimising OPcache settings, you can dramatically improve the performance of your Magento 2 web site. Follow this link—OPcache[12] —for further optimizations.

- MySQL and alternatives. Properly configured MySQL is among the most important enhancements to the performance of Magento 2. First of all, it requires the understanding of your hardware; then, you should know what settings to use. But MySQL is not a necessity, since these are two reliable substitutes: MariaDB and Percona. Follow this link—MySQL[13] —for further information.

- New Relic. A slow page is always a good reason to leave a webstore and never return again. Luckily, there are a ton of different monitoring tools developed for identifying the problem in a timely fashion, and one of them is New Relic. Follow this link—New Relic[14] —for further information.

---

[11]https://firebearstudio.com/blog/magento-2-extensions-reviewed-on-firebear.html
[12]https://firebearstudio.com/blog/magento-performance-ultimate-guide-mysql-opcache-cache-cdn-nginx.html#Zend%20PHP%20Accelerator%20configurations
[13]https://firebearstudio.com/blog/magento-performance-ultimate-guide-mysql-opcache-cache-cdn-nginx.html#Magento%20MySQL%20optimised%20configuration
[14]https://firebearstudio.com/blog/magento-performance-ultimate-guide-mysql-opcache-cache-cdn-nginx.html#Monitoring%20tools%20and%20analyzers

This was our short guide to Magento 2 performance. We are going to update it as soon as new information is available. For more tips related to Magento 2 development, check our Cookbook[15]. For other important information, visit this page: Everything about Magento 2 on Firebear[16].

---

[15]https://firebearstudio.com/blog/magento-2-developers-cookbook-useful-code-snip-pets-tips-notes.html
[16]https://firebearstudio.com/blog/the-ultimate-magento-2-tutorial.html

CHAPTER 12

Migration

After the launch of Magento 2, it is vital to understand how to migrate from Magento 1 to Magento 2. Since the migration is a complex process with lots of all possible aspects, you should know what to do with themes, extensions, data, and custom features. In this chapter, we've gathered all information about Magento 2 migration[1]. Below you will find useful migration tips as well as reliable Magento 2 migration tools.

Magento 2 Migration: Requirements

Migration elapse time is among key requirements. While critical for big projects, it is less important for small sites. For a big web site, migration could take from several hours to a few days.

Keep in mind that it shouldn't be necessary to take the site offline for too long. The problem is in performing a full bulk copy of the database. That takes too long. A variation of the catch-up phase is also required. This phase occurs after the main bulk copy and requires the offline phase.

It is important to place restrictions on operations that should not be performed during the migration. For instance, it is possible to place orders, but all the changes done by administrators are prohibited. It is also expected that developers are going to provide migration support for their extensions. There are two possible approaches to data migration for extensions. First of all, developers can provide the necessary documentation with the detailed tutorials about migration. There is also a possibility of a more flexible and pluggable framework that can automate the migration.

Magento 2 Migration: Current conditions

Both an export of database contents and an import into Magento 2 are too slow. The current design relies on a direct database-to-database data transfer.

A configuration file specifies which content should be copied from Magento 1 to the Magento 2 database. The official support went only to the recent Magento 1 releases. Earlier versions require the appropriate adjustment of the configuration file.

---

[1]https://firebearstudio.com/blog/migration-to-magento-2-plans-updates-tools-extensions-tutorials.html

V. Khliupko, *Magento 2 DIY*, DOI 10.1007/978-1-4842-2460-1_12

Besides simple table copies, PHP code is also able to be plugged into the process. It is required to perform more complicated data migration.

To capture changes to selected tables during the bulk copy, database triggers are used. All these changes are saved in a table for later use. To reduce the number of triggers, you should limit the administrator actions.

The migration tool also works with product images. Sites that do not rely on the default image storage may require some additional actions.

Magento 2 Migration: The migration procedure

1. Create database triggers, which are necessary to capture increment changes.

2. Run the data bulk copy.

3. Stop all changes and make the old site offline.

4. Perform catch-up changes.

5. Delete all triggers from the old database.

6. Turn the new Magento 2 site online.

Magento 2 Migration: More tips on migration to Magento 2

Hit the link and you will find a tutorial explaining Magento 2 migration. The material offers a lot of useful tips developed to help you with the migration to Magento 2.

Magento 2 Migration Tools

Below, you will find the most robust tools designed to make Magento 2 migration seamless. There are both official and third-party software solutions described in this section.

Code Migration Toolkit

A new tool that simplifies migration to Magento 2 has been developed. As members of the Magento community, we've been waiting for a new migration instrument aimed at modules since the first announcement of Magento 2, and finally we've got it. Dubbed the Magento Code Migration Toolkit, the software solution will essentially change the way you used to work with custom Magento extensions while trying to port them from 1.X to 2.0.

With the Magento Code Migration Toolkit, you get scripts that streamline the conversion of custom 1.x modules to Magento 2 by automating time-consuming processes. The software solution automatically converts such important things as module directory structure as well as PHP, config.xml, and layout.xml files.

Please note that the Magento Code Migration Toolkit requires some manual operations to be performed. For instance, conversion scripts must be run in the specified order. Besides, it is necessary to edit some files in the installation manually.

As for prerequisites, they are the following:

- PHP 5.5.x+

- cthe omposer package management software

- designated source, which is Magento 1.x

- target directories of Magento 2

The installation procedure and module migration process are described on the Magento Code Migration Toolkit page on GitHub.

Get Magento Code Migration Toolkit

Official Magento CE Data Migration Tool

Painless migration from Magento 1.x to Magento 2 is possible with Magento CE Data Migration Tool. Currently, the extension supports the following components: data, themes, extensions, customizations.

Magento 2 Data Migration Tool provides the ability to move store configurations, promotions, customers, products, and order data from Magento 1.x to Magento 2.

Please note that code is not ported due to its inability to be automated.

Still, there is no certain information about porting extensions. Check GitHub for the additional data. Developers are working hard with the community to provide the ability to port Magento Modules.

Magento 2 relies on an innovative approach to themes and customization. Thus, merchants and developers will need to change the existing products in order to get all the abilities of new shopping experiences. Don't forget to check official documentations for: themes, layouts, and customizations.

Magento CE Data Migration Tool works with Community Edition 1.9.1.0. Support for CE 1.6.x, CE 1.7.x, CE 1.8.x, CE 1.9.x is expected.

Prerequisites

It's important to comply with the requirements:

- Set up your Magento 2.0 in order to these system requirements[2].

- Set up the topology and design of a new system with your existing Magento 1.x system in mind.

- Please note that it is prohibited to start Magento 2.0 cron jobs.

- Back up your Magento 2 database after installation. Do it as soon as possible. You can also dump it.

---

[2]https://firebearstudio.com/blog/magento-2-system-requirements.html

- Magento CE Data Migration Tool should have a network connection to the databases of both Magento 1.x and Magento 2.

- The ports in your firewall should be opened. Provide your databases and the migration tool with the ability to communicate with each other.

- You can replicate your Magento 1.x database in order to provide redundancy in the event of unexpected issues.

- Migrate the existing 1.x custom code and extension to Magento 2.0.

- Ask providers of your extension if you've ported them successfully.

Download Magento CE Data Migration Tool

Testing Magento 2 Data Migration Tool

There is a good post about Magento 2 Data Migration Tool on Inchoo. The author describes current opportunities and limitations introduced in the tool. Unfortunately, the solution for data migration to Magento 2 is far from perfect. It still does not provide support for themes and customizations, for instance. Therefore, get ready for tons of manual work while migrating to Magento 2. Firebear members believe that one day this process will be seamless, but not today. You can read more about Testing Magento 2 Data Migration Tool here.

Magento 2 DB Migration

This script is designed to migrate database from Magento 1.8 or 1.9 to Magento 2 beta5. Keep in mind that this tool comes with no warranty. In addition, this module should be adapted for each new version of Magento 2.

Pay attention to the fact that Magento 2 provides a lot of changes to the code. As a result, more internal refactoring will be necessary in the future.

Magento 2 DB Migration on GitHub

Magento 2 Data Migration Tool by Ubertheme

This is another solution, designed to help you with migration to Magento 2. The process is described at GitHub. You can also find all the necessary requirements there.

Magento 2 Data Migration Tool on GitHub

CHAPTER 13

■ ■ ■

Generating New Sales

The newcomers in the field of e-commerce often tend to have problems with gaining enough traffic to their web sites. It is quite difficult to attract customers if nobody even knows about your existence. Since making profit online requires a lot of time, investments, planning, and management, you have to be patient and consistent to get your web site out of the Google search abyss and increase your web site traffic. In this chapter, we'll shed light on the most effective ways of sales generation in the context of a successful marketing campaign.

Evaluate your marketing campaign

With the e-commerce industry exceeding $294 billion of profit in 2014, it is not surprising that digital commerce is worth being called a competitive market. This, however, must call for more actions, because retailers, who think that their marketing strategy can bring money steadily for years, are going to lose everything just within several months. E-commerce marketing nowadays is a tough job requiring a lot of effort.

The most effective way of maintaining your business on the highest level is a constant control over the success of your current strategies and, if they fail in fulfilling a plan, the invention of better ones. Therefore, get ready for an intensive study of planning, implementing, and evaluating your marketing campaigns.

1. Understand your aims.

    If you're not really sure what you want to reach by your marketing campaign, you will not succeed in it anyway. Even if you spend a great amount of money on numerous ads believing that this is a successful campaign, you're wrong. Thus, it's important to make a clear plan of what you want to achieve by your strategy. For instance:

    - Reach the amount of 1,000 orders per month.

    - Obtain 500 new customers.

    - Increase the growth of revenues by 30%.

2.   Identify metrics for measuring your campaign.

At the end of the first period, you can start measuring the results of a current strategy. For each aim established at the beginning, you will have to utilize appropriate metrics to calculate their value. For instance, if your aim was to gain more sales to your web site, the following rates must be considered:

- average amount of product page views

- percentage ratio of users that purchased your products to all users that viewed your web site during a certain period

- sum of total revenue

3.   Implement comfortable metrics tracking.

Having your ads active allows you to easily monitor the amount of visitors coming to your web site and mostly all the activities performed by these visitors through the toolkit of your particular ad campaign.

Thus, you're open to control all stages of a potential purchase from the very first view of a page to a complete product purchase. In fact, by using your ad stats you will get the exact rates for performing final calculations. For example, to calculate an overall conversion rate of a particular product, you may simply divide the number of its purchases by the amount of product page views for a given period.

4.   Be original with every media representation of your site.

For each ad campaign, you should use different visual solutions to perfectly suit the social environment you want to integrate your web site with. For instance, if you create an ad on Facebook, make sure to use unusual color scheme or imagery which is likely to attract the major audience of the network to your web site. Sometimes you will even have to be minimalistic if you don't want to spoil impressions of your customers.

5.   Use UTM links to direct users to the most suitable page.

If you create ads on several web sites or platforms, it would be nice if you could see which of them brings the greatest amount of customers. Thus, you can utilize so-called UTM links which are basically specific parameters assigned to the main link. They can help you with tracking the amount of clicks performed with every ad as well as analyzing their efficiency in your primary campaign.

There are numerous tools for creating UTM links, such as Google URL Builder and Terminus, but while the former is considered to be relatively easy to use, the latter contains a set of more advanced settings for experienced retailers.

The main UTM parameters for adjusting to an ad link are:

- source (web site at which your ad is located, e.g., Facebook);

- medium (variation of your banner, e.g., banner variation 1);

- campaign (name of your ad campaign, e.g., autumn collection).

The result should looks as follows:

```
http://yoursite.com/blog-post-fall-collection/?
utm_source=facebook&utm_medium=bannerverision1&
utm_- campaign=autumncollection
```

Add such link to all your ads and publish it only if you're sure that it works properly.

6. Run some tests before publishing your ads.

It is important to test how UTM links work and whether they direct users to the right place. Try to produce all the actions of a potential customer starting with clicking on ads, browsing various product pages and ending with check-out. Then, go to your tracking page and see whether the metrics change their values. If everything is fine, proceed to the next step.

7. See the results.

In order to provide yourself with a convenient way of tracking your metrics, you can use several handy tools that will help you understand whether your goals are achievable. The best solutions are listed below:

- KISSmetrics—a flexible medium for effective tracking of major campaign rates;

- Google Analytics—good at dealing with UTM links;

- Converto—a more advanced tool which offers the ability to analyze the efficiency of all your ads and redirect your resources to more profitable channels.

Keep in mind that even if your campaign fails, with these analytical add-ons at hand you should identify which rates appeared to be insufficient and to calculate current losses. Using official ad tools on your advertising channels is also possible, but it often happens that rate values are different from what you might expect.

8. Make a conclusion and prepare for further campaigns.

However, getting results is not your final destination yet. In addition to evaluating your campaign achievements, you should analyze each of your advertising channels to define which of them gained the biggest audience. For instance, you may discover that Facebook gave you 500 page views, among which 50 were purchases. Thus, we can suggest that Facebook is likely to be effective for attracting customers, but certain modifications of your ad campaign on this platform are required. If your Twitter ad campaign brought you just 200 page views, but 150 of those still ended up with completing an order, this ad source is worth being invested. Those ad sources that brought you nothing but a few page views for the whole period should be discarded.

Finally, learn all your achievements and failures from the current marketing strategy and next time apply this knowledge for getting your business to the first positions on the e-commerce market.

The main traffic sources

As a retailer, you might be curious about what traffic sources can bring you the desired number of customers. In fact, everything depends on the size of your business. For instance, in case of a small store it is not profitable to rely on direct traffic, so you'll have to look for other alternatives to achieve your marketing goals. Let's look at some traffic sources and define their pros and cons.

Direct traffic

Direct traffic is a flow of users who come to your web site by typing in the direct URL address in their browsers. To make this source valuable for you, it is important to become a popular brand offline and provide people with the ability to engage with you and your products by actually going to your brick-and-mortar stores. In this case, all the investments must be made for a high-quality PR scheme and opening of an offline store chain. The principle disadvantage of this source is that it can only bring 10-15% of visitors. Besides, if you're generally doing well with your offline business, you can look for more advanced ways of driving extra traffic to your online store.

E-mail marketing

This traffic source is considered to be one of the cheapest ones. Furthermore, it can be used for all possible kinds of business. The main priority of e-mail marketing is the ability to keep in touch with the existing customers and encourage them to make more purchases from your online store. This traffic source requires the following:

- Sufficient database volume

  This means that you should have an adequate number of
  users to whom you will send your e-mails. You can either buy
  data or build it yourself. Buying data can be fast and easy, but
  it does not guarantee that users will react. After all, they don't
  know you, so you're likely to be marked as spam. Building
  your own e-mail list may seem more reasonable, but it
  usually takes a good deal of time to attract enough customers,
  especially if you've just started your business. However, you
  can use organic ways to encourage visitors to share their
  e-mail addresses with you. This includes creating visual
  incentives—for instance, offering bargains to your items to
  subscribed users.

- Frequent e-mail delivery

  Any type of e-mail marketing campaign suggests that you
  should provide a regular e-mail delivery to your contact list
  users. However, this regularity should not exceed three emails
  a month, because frequent e-mailing will cause people, as
  well as e-mail services, to consider you as a spammer. When
  a smart e-mail service, such as Gmail, identifies you as a
  spammer, your e-mails are automatically sent to a spam
  folder, which prevents a recipient from even noticing it. Thus,
  you should be consistent but unobtrusive while gaining
  traffic.

- Appropriate quality of e-mail content

  When it comes to building up content for your e-mails, use
  the information which can be found on only your web site.
  Goods and prices that don't exist on your Magento 2 store
  will disappoint potential customers. Besides, don't make your
  e-mails too long. Write only about the most relevant things
  that can make people interested in what you are doing. It's
  often useful to combine textual content with catchy images
  to make it more user-friendly. For instance, you can write 4-5
  sentences to describe your content and then support them
  with a relevant picture representing your offer. Apart from the
  things mentioned above, we would like to recommend adding
  corresponding links to your web site.

Thus, you should manage e-mail marketing during the first days of your web site
existence. Providing yourself with an opportunity to bring your customers back at any
particular time can double your conversions and create friendly relationships between
you and your customers. Despite the fact that e-mail marketing accounts for 10-30% of
visitors, it won't work for acquiring new customers, because you are unlikely to interest
people who have never purchased your products.

Apart from independent research and testing opportunities of your e-mail marketing campaigns, you can also utilize services of specialized e-mail marketing providers. They can consult with you (often for free) and give useful advice on how to get along with this source of traffic. The price for paid services varies a lot depending on whether you want to save your time and make the whole process run automatically or manage everything yourself. Such a service which combines a set of valuable e-commerce features with a reasonable price is MailChimp.

MailChimp

For a minimum of $10 per month, you can get high-end e-mail content that will be appealing to your customers. Moreover, you can also take advantage of regular analytics reports that will inform you about the current progress of your e-mail campaign. With MailChimp's functionality, you will be able to easily improve your marketing performance by utilizing a set of its useful features, such as:

- E-mail Designer

    E-mail Designer is an all-in-one editor which is based on the drag-and-drop principle. It can be managed from a PC and laptop as well as from a tablet or smartphone. Its built-in toolkit allows you to:

    1. edit and resize images;

    2. effectively interact with your team no matter where you are;

    3. conduct a testing campaign before actually launching it;

    4. store and retrieve your files in a specialized file manager;

    5. automatically verify every link you submit to e-mails.

- E-mail templates

    MailChimp offers a smart collection of predesigned templates which you can use if you lack enough time or experience for creating a good-looking design. So the only thing you have to do is submit the content and check how it looks with each particular template. In case you intend to code your own e-mail template, there is the E-mail Template Reference option that has a lot of useful information and recommendations on how to make a nice and working template for a successful e-mail marketing scheme.

- Smart Reports

    When your campaign is finally on the go, you can instantly start monitoring its performance through MailChimp's smart reports, which provide you with detailed data such as the number of newly subscribed users, URL visits, and impressions.

- Integration with e-commerce platforms

If you want to reach various categories of customers with equal efficiency, you will need to import all user data to your MailChimp account. Take into consideration that the service supports integration with Google Analytics, Magento and Shopify.

There are three plans available for acquisition on MailChimp: Entrepreneur, Growing Business, and High Volume Sender.

The Entrepreneur package is free of charge and has no expiration date. You can send a fixed number of 12,000 e-mails to 2,000 users each month. Also, you can sort your customer list out to manage e-mail delivery to target groups of customers. The plan supports e-commerce integration and the access to the pack of ready-to-use e-mail templates. The downside of this plan consists of the lack of support for analytical tools for monitoring the coming web site traffic. The Entrepreneur package is intended for small businesses that don't have a large audience; this guarantees that every user will receive at least one e-mail per month. If you acquire more than 2,000 users, you will need to subscribe to a paid plan which widens the functionality of your account and allows you to send an unlimited number of messages. It will cost you only $10 per month.

The Growing Business plan supports unlimited monthly e-mail delivery to 600,000 subscribers. You can use MailChimp's official web site[1] for calculating an actual amount of money required for a given number of users per month. For instance, a plan for up to 5,000 users will cost you $50, while a plan for 10,000 will cost you $75. The same pricing works for the High Volume Sender package as well. The plan supports customer list segmentation and integration with e-commerce platforms. Additionally, you get an opportunity to manage your team work by using E-mail Designer and have a regularly available consulting team of experts to help you adapt the MailChimp system within your e-commerce store.

The High Volume Seller package suits large corporations with wide audiences (600,000 customers). It offers the ability to send billions of e-mails per month. You can automatically adjust your delivery due to provider responses and protect data with a two-factor authentication process, SOC II and PCI DSS certifications and security alerts. There is also access to a full API provided with detailed documentation and user guides. In addition, the package features multi-user accounts for agencies to manage their cooperative engagement and interaction with clients.

Magento 2 MailChimp Integration[2]

Organic search engine results

These are results displayed to a user after he enters a search request. The first appearing results usually contain the most relevant information, which is more likely to meet search requirements. That's why organic search results almost never include advertising links in the top results. Even Google tries to divide relevant result links from ads, putting the former in the first place and moving the latter down to the lower positions. This means that placing your web site among the first positions requires high popularity among people or original and rare products and services which won't create excessive competitiveness on the Internet. In addition to the things mentioned above, you need an effective SEO strategy.

In general, organic search results bring from 10% to 30% of visitors on a regular basis.

---

[1] http://goo.gl/wmvbYp
[2] http://store.ebizmarts.com/magemonkey-magento2.html

Paid search results

Paid search results, if used properly, can provide you with up to 50% of visitors, which is the highest rate among all traffic drivers. This source of customers usually requires a sufficient number of resources to be spent, since advertising tends to become more and more complicated for attracting people's attention. In a perfect scenario, you should be able to invest in both offline and online stores to gain maximum profit from the paid search. Online marketing campaigns usually include the following methods: SEO, Pay Per Click ads, and affiliate marketing.

1. Search Engine Optimization

    This technique is considered to be the most popular for increasing web site traffic because it can attain crazy numbers of visits. Please note that it usually takes months until SEO strategy shows its results, so you will need consistency and patience to gain the desired traffic flow to your web site.

    Although the main SEO optimizations are described in the first chapter of this book, we'd like to draw your attention to this complicated process once again. The main issue related to search engine optimization is content, which means that you will have to work on the effectiveness of your texts and product listings. The whole procedure includes:

    - Check and improve your product categories. Make sure that every product contains a sufficient amount of key-words (words and word-phrases that users are likely to type in when they search for these products on Google or any other search engine). Then, include these keywords in the most noticeable places of your web site: headers, item descriptions, image names, internal links, and body text itself.

    - Make your text authentic. Work with professional writers that will make your descriptions, articles, and other text pieces readable and informative for potential customers. Your main aim is to put the most relevant information in proper order.

    - Utilize landing pages. Originally, a landing page is a single web site page that contains relevant and crucial data for a viewer. For instance, you can create a customer-specific link that will direct a person from a search results page or an ad towards a certain product page containing a description, characteristics, and price. This is likely to motivate a user for a purchase.

    - Ask bloggers and other retailers to mention your store on their web sites. This part is the most difficult one, because further success of your marketing campaign becomes in some sense dependant on whether your web site URL appears on other blogs or pages. It makes sense to be friendly in order to become successful.

    - Submit your web site to various directories. Google, Bing, and Business.com must be your primary candidates.

2. Pay Per Click advertising

The Pay Per Click ads are really good at increasing your web site traffic faster than any other alternative solutions. This technology allows you to buy visitors on the web sites where you place your ads. Once users click on your ad, they are instantly redirected to your web site. As an advertiser, you have to pay to web sites owners for every single click.

The most popular Pay Per Click management service is Google AdWords which can bring you about 70% of paid search visitors. But before using it you should learn all the opportunities related to this Pay Per Click solution. Note that the service is full of other retailers many of whom occupy the top positions in search results.

- Analyze how many retailers sell the same goods as you.

- Make the most powerful set of keywords for your product ads.

- Work on the appearance of your ads (design, colors, images, etc.)

- Adjust retargeting ads for your web site. Retargeting ads are basically the same old ads but their aim is to track your web site visitors after they have left a web site page. For instance, when a person goes to your web site, nothing happens, but as soon as he or she proceeds to other web sites, your ad will be displayed on each of these sites.

- Note that cost-per-click or CPC options are always better than cost-per-mille or CPM options. Don't pay for viewers—pay for their actions, especially if your goal is to capture leads.

- Your ads should have URLs with a unique tracking token. Thus, you will be able to test them and evaluate their effectiveness. Without this information you will never optimize your ROI.

- The writing style of your landing page and an advertisement on social media should correspond to one another. At least try to use the same language, otherwise you'll confuse your customers.

- Provide high-quality content: avoid typos (if they are not a part of your creative campaign), make sure every image has a proper size, check if every URL goes to the right landing pages.

- Use A/B testing and try out different types of ads. This will help you choose better options and get the most out of your PPC campaign.

It is also worth mentioning that Pay Per Click management works in social network environments including Twitter, Youtube, and Facebook. An even more surprising fact is that you can use Pay Per Click ads on mobile devices.

3. Affiliate Marketing

    Affiliate marketing includes interaction with third-party web sites that will definitely come in handy when it comes to driving traffic to your store. Basically, these sites use the same methods as those mentioned above for selling your products "on their territory," but it will require extra expenditures (about 10%) from every sale they make. The most reliable affiliate web sites are Affiliate Window, Linkshare, and Webgain.

    Unfortunately, dealing with affiliates will involve additional investments into the development of specific data feeds obtained from your product database. These data feeds will be integrated into the affiliate's own database to enable ordering of your products on their web site. Moreover, additional banners and newsletters that will be distinguishable from those you use on other advertising platforms are required. Keep in mind that you can track user activity on affiliate web sites by using Google Analytics platform.

The best Magento 2 affiliate and referral modules

Here is a set of Magento 2 extensions aimed at simplifying the process of finding and cooperating with affiliates and referrals. Each affiliate module serves different purposes, so be sure to pick up the one that you really need.

Mirasvit Reward Points + Referral program for Magento 2

Currently, only Mirasvit offers a referral Magento 2 extension. It is a flexible tool designed for implementing loyalty programs on your Magento 2 storefront. Reward Points + Referral Program appreciates your clients every time they do something good for your e-commerce business. Thus, by encouraging your shoppers, you turn them into loyal customers and returning buyers who invite their friends to shop on your web site.

As a store owner, you can reward your visitors for:

*referring friends to your Magento 2 store; *purchasing several items simultaneously; *reviewing products; *buying specific products; *placing votes; *signing up; *telling about your store on social networks.

There is also an opportunity to reward someone in case of a birthday. As for the back end opportunities, this referral Magento 2 extension allows you to create and manage flexible earning and spending rules. Besides, you can create rules for notifications, add points manually, and change point statuses.

And it is necessary to mention three types of earning rules. First of all, you can create product-based rules. Then, the module provides an opportunity to make some behavior-based rules. And finally, you can create cart-based rules.

More about Mirasvit Reward Points Referral Magento 2 Extension[3]

---

[3]https://firebearstudio.com/blog/mirasvit-reward-points-referral-program-magento-2-and-1-review.html

Other useful traffic-driving techniques...

...to use on your web site

1. Simplified checkout

    Approximately 50% of all abandoned check-out processes are caused by complex and unfriendly shopping experiences. The more complex and lengthy this process is, the less inclined customers are to make a purchase.. To increase sales, try to simplify the checkout experience:

    - Choose the most user-friendly template for your shopping cart options.

    - Simplify a sign-in process for returning customers.

    - Reduce overall checkout time by uniting closely-related data in one checkout step.

2. Full shipping information

    This concerns mostly information about shipping costs. When a customer literally bumps into a shipping price at the final step of his or her order completion, it often spoils a previously settled positive mood. The same happens when a shipping price is not exact, with a myriad of additional conditions and restrictions suggesting that the final sum is subject to vary significantly. Therefore, complex shipping costs and conditions increase the number of failed check-out processes.

    The most reliable solution in this case is to put shipping information at the first steps of your checkout procedure and make the price as low as possible to avoid discouraging positive expectations from customers.

3. Mobile-friendly environment

    There is almost nobody who doesn't have access to a mobile device these days, and there are a huge number of people that spend much more time surfing the Internet from their smartphones and tablets rather than laptops or computers. This means you must adapt to the universal trend and optimize your web site for smartphones and tablets. Providing your customers with an intuitive mobile shopping experience will greatly increase your traffic and sales.

4. Giveaways

    Everybody likes getting things for free, and you can use this
    tendency to attract the attention of potential customers. It
    can be anything ranging from supporting mobile apps and
    extensions to handy accessories and packaging services.

5. Feedback opportunities

    About 80% of all customers tend to make their purchasing
    decisions based on reviews they read on retail web sites. The
    most important thing is that reviews and recommendations
    can be used by consumers in order to provide additional
    information about your products to their colleagues and
    friends, making them even more valuable for retailers.
    Moreover, having reviews available makes your web site
    generally more reliable in comparison with those that don't
    have this option. But in order to make it more effective, don't
    hesitate to ask your customers for feedback. Not everyone is
    apt to leave it after purchasing a product.

    Although reviews can be positive or negative, you must be
    ready to see both types on your web site. It's not always the
    case that your products or services are bad, though. But it
    doesn't matter what the reason for a bad feedback is. Think of
    it as a factor that can help you boost your market performance
    and increase overall traffic to your web site.

    These techniques are also important when estimating the
    conversion rate of your web site. Abandoned shopping
    carts, zero returns from e-mail campaigns, and absence of
    feedback from your customers are the main factors affecting
    your conversion rate. Because this value plays the main part
    in determining how good your relationships with existing
    customers are, you will also have to be ready to take steps
    towards conversion rate optimization strategy.

...to use outside of your web site

1. Don't give up on traditional advertising.

    Although we live in the age of computers, it doesn't mean we
    cannot use old-school methods anymore. It also concerns
    advertising, however controversial this sphere may be.
    Traditional advertising can be still actualized through
    magazines, newspapers, direct mail marketing, radio stations,
    TV, and even billboards. Moreover, it can also increase your
    web site traffic!

Consider such giants as Zappos, Diapers.com, Bonobos, and Amazon. Despite the fact that they are hugely popular on the Internet, these companies still rely on traditional advertising to keep their sales and web site views high.

2. Entertain your customers.

Using entertainment as a source of new traffic may seem an odd thing, but it really works. Try to turn on your imagination and think of various content which could bring you more customers since it is funny. One of the most commonly used entertaining elements in the sphere of e-commerce is a viral video. Viral videos are made by many world-famous brands, and their efficiency is considered to be proved due to enormous success they achieve afterwards. Some brands even adjust themselves to YouTube and create official channels where they promote their products by introducing them in a row of funny or creative video series.

3. Take part in offline events.

This might be especially useful if you have only an online store which has been recently launched. Apart from using traditional ways of e-commerce marketing, you can simply attend various offline fairs and other sales events to get people acquainted with your products and services. Accompany your attendance with original and colorful leaflets and product samples. Use all possible ways to make people visit your online store.

4. Expose your business to other e-commerce platforms.

If you don't yet feel stable enough with traffic, don't hesitate to promote your products on bigger e-commerce platforms such as Amazon and eBay. Millions of people visit these sites every day, so it's likely that they will stumble upon your products for being original, cheap, or both.

5. Use banner ads.

This is another efficient technique for driving traffic to your Magento 2 web site. Since it is quite complicated, we've decided to devote a separate part of this chapter to banner ads. You can check it out below.

Banner Ads

This type of advertisement must be familiar to every e-commerce retailer, but many of them do not consider it to be as effective as previously thought. Firstly, because modern users are highly knowledgeable about computers and specifically the Internet, it's not that easy to attract their attention anymore. The only reaction people experience when seeing an ad is utter irritation, because their presence on a web site is dictated by the need to read/watch something interesting or communicate with somebody rather than to click on some crazy-colored suspicious banners. As a result, retailers develop more original approaches and switch to more complicated banners, but the strategy still crashes due to ad blocking software, which is popular among users all over the world. In spite of these unpleasant facts about banner ads, there is still a green light for retailers to use them for driving traffic to their web sites. Below we will tell you how to use them properly.

How to use

Considering current problems related to banner ads, you may come to the conclusion that it's almost impossible to profit from using them. But there are key conditions which are to be observed in order to make your banner ads work:

- Define a list of web sites relevant for your audience. If you think that having an ad everywhere can improve your situation, you're highly mistaken.

- Spend more time on making your ads creative. Creativity still attracts attention, as it can be beautiful, entertaining, smart, and eye-catching.

- Make some tests before submitting your banner ad. If it does not work properly or cannot be monitored from tracking services, it's better to fix all these problems before investing in it.

- Contact potential banner ad publishers directly. Being able to communicate with web site owners is a useful skill that provides the most favorable advertising conditions. You should sound natural and generous. These owners are basically the influencers of your products, so the more contacts you have, the more successful your banner ad campaign is.

- Be aware of the F-shaped view pattern. This is a general page view pattern and a common feature for everyone browsing the Internet. According to it, users tend to look at the top of a page first, then explore the content itself starting from a left side, proceeding to a right side and then back, then go to the middle, do the same left-right manipulations, and so on. You can use the knowledge of the F-shaped pattern to find the best place for your banner ads. Accordingly, it will be either the top of the page, or its left side. Unfortunately, when dealing with ad publishers, you will have to rely on their own ad placement priorities.

- Enhance your landing pages, since they are important for all kinds of online ads due to the ability to direct users to the most desirable places of your web site, either already existing or newly created ones. The main purpose of landing pages is to incline users to buy your goods. Thus, it's up to you which place on your Magento 2 store will be a landing page.

Where to buy

Basically, you will have to choose among two kinds of banner ads sources: individual publishers or ad networks.

Individual publishers

If you already have a list of potential banner ad publishers dealing with a similar market segment, go and contact their owners or advertising operators. Learn their prices and subscription conditions and decide how long you are going to work with them. Keep in mind that if you advertise on a particular web site for a long time, you may become easily recognizable by its audience and therefore more trustful. Therefore, you can obtain a stable number of loyal customers. But it does not mean that you don't have to update your ads and their design regularly.

Ad networks

Ad networks are not niche-specific banner ad resources, but can be considered as a competitive alternative to direct ad publishers. Ad networks are usually a third party that chooses web sites to publish your banner ads on. Thus, they can save you time performing all the work instead of you. As for the bad side, it is harder to drive traffic to your store, and you are not able to communicate with publishers directly. The most popular ad network is AdWords.

AdWords

AdWords is Google's official advertising program that is commonly used by businesses all over the world. It's the first thing you're advised to try in your never-ceasing attempt to get more traffic to your web site. With the help of this program you can manage your ads and choose the most appealing web sites to place them on. The main advantage of the service is its relatively low cost and easy break-up procedure. In addition, you can adjust the program so that your ads are seen only by local users, especially when you tend to attract more customers to your physical store. You also can place your ad right on a Google results page; therefore, users can go directly to a product page they get interested in.

How it functions

Keyword is a basic element of the AdWords toolkit that allows you to place your web site ads near the first positions of a Google search results list. You should simply create a range of the most relevant keywords based on your business activity or products. Be specific when choosing the most important keywords and give priority to two to three word phrases rather than simple words.

It is also important to mention that AdWords can show your ads on other web sites sharing Google-owned properties (like YouTube) as well as Google's partner sites (like NYTimes.com or Families.com). The place on the web site used for showing your ad is called placement.

AdRank is an additional value of AdWords that is used to determine your ad's position on a web site or among search results. It also determines whether your ad will be displayed at all. You should remember, though, that the main factors defining an ad's location are the amount of bids you offer (the sum you're ready to spend) and the quality of your ad. As a result, the first and the most prominent positions in the list will be given to the ads with highest bids and quality. What's even more interesting about AdRank is its ability to recalculate processing data and update positions of ads according to their current value.

As for bids and ad/web site quality, their value varies depending on the kind of ads you use as well as the kind of web site you have. Note that your actual bid is closely connected to your maximum cost-per- click bid, which is the maximum amount you could pay per one click. However, usually you're charged less. Everything depends on the quality of your ad (which is calculated according to the expected number of potential clicks), ad relevance and landing page availability. Ad auction determines the maximum cost-per-click bid which is required to keep your ad at a given position.

How to fit into budget

One of the main drawbacks of AdWords lies in its competitiveness, i.e., constant competition among retailers for getting the best ad positions. The more money you offer, the more chances you get to appear among the first positions and, accordingly, get more clicks to your web site. Thus, a steady-developing retailer has to be able to invest at least $2,000-5,000 a month in an ordinary AdWords campaign. Nonetheless, buying web site traffic consists of more than clicks. The better retailer you are, the more bids you're required to offer. So before starting your cooperation with AdWords, take the following into account:

- How much money are you ready to spend for a single day of your advertising campaign? Days are more relevant than weeks or months because you cannot predict how long your ad will bring you enough profit.

- Will you vary your daily bid into parts by bidding in specific times of a day? This ad scheduling is very useful and cost-saving if you know when your web site experiences the best-selling hours.

- Is your quality score high enough to be worth risking? If you're not sure about the relevance of your keywords and the quality of your ad and landing page, it's better to invest in their improvement first.

How to structure your ad campaign

Depending on the kind of ads you have, your approaches to an AdWords campaign will vary. Product ads usually tend to work out provided they are divided into definite categories; for instance, furniture products are better structured when categorized into beds, chairs, tables, and so on. Furthermore, you can specify each category by introducing single-size beds and double-size beds. That will make your ads more specific for potential customers, and will clarify which products are more popular than others.

How to manage your resources

Working with AdWords requires certain time expenditures as well. The more developed retailer you are, the more profound ad campaign planning you should do. To buy internet traffic simply by putting some money into it is never enough. Using text ads is indeed easier, but it's evident that for a range of products you should work on its proper listing in AdWords webpages, manage regular updates of assortment and price, and automate submissions to Google Merchant Center. These hard tasks often require hiring corresponding specialists, but the results will definitely be worth it.

How to launch an AdWords campaign

Below, we will shed light on launching an ordinary AdWords campaign for your Magento 2 web site. Let's start with some basic aspects, such as your AdWords account.

Create an account in AdWords

1. First, visit AdWords' main page[4] and choose Try AdWords Now.

2. If you already have a Google account, then you can simply sign in with the existing login and password; otherwise, tick "I do not use these services" and enter your e-mail address as well as a relatively strong password. Then solve a captcha and create an account.

3. Select your country, timezone, and currency you'd like to deal with. Google's billing will highly depend on this information. Remember that after submitting this data you will not be able to change it.

4. Click Continue and verify your account through the link sent to your e-mail address.

Choose your ad campaign

Each campaign can be run on the same or various AdWords settings. It's up to your tastes and possibilities. There are three basic settings areas:

- budget and bid amount

- optional elements that can be adjusted to the main ad structure through ad extensions

- specification of places where you want your ads to appear

---

[4]http://www.google.co.uk/adwords/

Now, it's time to look through settings:

1. Campaign name. This name will only be visible to you, but it would be great if you specify it according to your actual business goals. It's not recommended to use default Google names in order to be able to find a particular campaign afterwards.

2. Type. Here you can specify what kind of ads you're going to create. For novices in advertising it's reasonable to select the "Search Network with Display Select" type of a campaign that allows you to gain access to the most popular ad placements. You can also choose a subtype of your campaign which determines the range of settings you will use for making an ad. The Standard subtype is preferred when you're a newbie.

3. Networks. You can choose either Google Search Network or Google Display Network to manage the appearance of your ad on other web sites. The first option implies that your ads will be shown on Google-related web sites including YouTube and AOL, and the second option enables your ads to be shown on other web sites having partnership with Google.

4. Devices. You can work on this option later when you decide to optimize your ads for tablets and mobile devices.

5. Locations and Languages. Here you can choose an appropriate language for your ads, as well as a location that will provide only targeted location users with the ability to see your ads.

6. Bidding and budget. You can insert bids manually or delegate them with the help of this option. Remember that your default bid represents the maximum amount you're ready to pay for your ad's placement, while budget shows how much you really intend to spend for every day of your campaign.

7. Ad extensions. This category contains additional settings including the placement of links to your web site, your local store address, or phone number.

8. Advanced Settings. Here you will find optional settings aimed at displaying your ads on your customers' screens at the most appropriate time. This category features different schedules, such as the program of your campaign or times ads appear each day.

Create a new campaign.

1. Click on "Create your first campaign."

2. You'll be directed to the "Select Campaign Settings" page where you can set up all the previously mentioned categories.

3. At the end, don't forget to click on "Save and Continue." Later you'll be able to edit most of the settings.

Ad Groups

After you're done with settings, you will be automatically introduced to the "Create ad and keywords" page. It is possible to create an ad group here and use it as a part of a more general ad campaign.

Each ad campaign includes one or multiple ad groups depending on the type selected in Campaign Settings. Each group consists of an ad, specialized keyword set, and bids for its placement. With certain keywords for every ad group, you enhance the relevance of your ads in a list of search results. Therefore, an ad group should correspond to a particular type of product you offer. After creating an ad group, you can proceed to managing ads themselves.

Ads

There are different formats of ads available for your ad campaigns. Regardless of the format, it is required to create a separate range of keywords for each of them. The available ad formats vary from text and image ads to video and mobile ads.

Let's have a look at the simplest text ad.

1. Choose "Create an ad" and click on "Text ad."

2. Fill in the spaces by writing your headline, description, display URL (your homepage), and landing page. Note that both links have to belong to the same domain.

3. Type in your keywords in the appropriate section. The recommended minimum of keywords is 10-20.

4. Click "Save and Continue to billing" to activate your campaign.

Billing information

After you've created your first ad, you will be asked to fill in billing information. Follow these steps:

1. Select the country of your billing address; then you will see additional settings available for your country. Input additional information.

2. Choose your payment method: backup credit card for automated payments (after your ads have been displayed) or a manual payment method (before your ads have been displayed). Please note that there are some restrictions related to certain countries.

3. If you chose backup credit card payment, you don't have to perform any additional actions. Otherwise, you can pay for your first bid in "Settings > Billing" by choosing "Make a payment." Don't forget to choose the amount of a bid.

4. Now, you should provide additional payment information.

5. Save input data.

Creating a shopping campaign

The format of an ad campaign is valuable when you have a store with various product items. Ads of such format usually include an image, name, description, price, and landing page leading towards a product page on your web site. To enable shopping campaigns for your AdWords account, submit your product information in Google Merchant Center. Consider that a shopping campaign is especially useful when you are targeting specific users.

Setup

1. Click on "Campaigns" and then "Campaign > Shopping"

2. You will be forwarded to the "Campaign Settings" page. Type the name of your campaign in the first place.

3. Select your country and add Merchant ID information.

4. In the "Country of Sale" field select the country where your products are sold.

5. Then you can manage optional settings in "Shopping Settings (advanced):"

   • Choose a "campaign priority" value in case of several shopping campaigns promoting the same product.

   • "Inventory filter" will allow you to limit the number of product items you'd like to advertise.

   • You can also activate "Local Inventory Ads" for your Local Products feed to Merchant Center.

- In "Locations" you can choose countries to display your ads in.

- "Bid strategy" allows you to adjust bidding options. If you set bids manually, use default parameters. For conversion tracking, choose enhanced cost-per-click (ECPC).

6. Save these settings.

AdWords conversion pixel

AdWords provides its users with an opportunity to track their conversion rates based on customers' interaction with your Magento 2 web site. This includes the number of ad clicks, product page views, app downloads, order check-outs, etc. Conversion tracking also features all the necessary tools for maximizing profit from you ad campaigns and reducing overall expenses. In addition, it sheds light on how good your ads are. The key element of AdWords conversion tracking is the conversion pixel tool which is basically a 1x1 pixel image placed on one or several web site pages through a piece of code that you can copy and paste as a part of your primary ad campaign. This pixel effectively reacts on every activity on your web site including:

- ad clicks from affiliate web sites;

- checkout button clicks on a checkout confirmation page;

- clicks on referral URLs leading from your store, which allows you to track visitors even when they leave your page.

Despite the fact that Magento 2 does not support AdWords conversion tracking out-of-the-box, there are a lot of third-party possibilities for effective integration. For instance, here[5] you can find a handy module written in JavaScript. Its primary role is tracking conversions from a checkout/success page of Magento 2 stores.

Here is a list of other useful guides and articles that would help you boost your AdWords experience:

- Official Google AdWords guide[6]

- Pay for Google AdWords[7]

- 5 E-commerce AdWords Tips from an ex-Googler[8]

- Search Advertising 101 - Your Guide to Google AdWords[9]

- How to Start Your AdWords Well[10]

- 12 Rules For Maximizing conversions from AdWords[11]

---

[5]http://goo.gl/fWhkSj
[6]https://goo.gl/axrg2U
[7]https://goo.gl/BRkeIW
[8]https://goo.gl/quzOSM
[9]https://goo.gl/txIGU1
[10]https://goo.gl/EUXKcC
[11]http://goo.gl/voIgF8

Alternatives to Google AdWords

Many retailers are accustomed to think that Google Adwords is the most effective Pay-Per-Click management service for driving more traffic to web sites. However, it may often be not that efficient and even harmful for your business, especially if you're a new entrepreneur. The problem is that you cannot realize the consequences until you invest in an AdWords campaign. Thus, you are facing the following:

- Rivalry. Being especially popular among large and highly developed companies, the AdWords platform makes it impossible for small businesses to be competitive. You will have to invest more and more just to be able to provide your ads with the best working keywords. With such cost-intensity, you're likely to burn out at the very beginning of your campaign.

- Time wasting. As an e-commerce newcomer, you won't be really knowledgeable in all the specifics of AdWords, so you will have to spend some time on getting acquainted with the toolkit. But such experiments are risky, because, again, you spend your money on them, and don't know any end results.

- Vague bidding system. AdWords has a quite intricate system of money distribution. Although you can control the amount of bids you submit for you campaign and even invest as little or much as you can, you will spend much time trying to find out where your money eventually goes. Moreover, if you fail to be attentive and forget to set a proper management over your bids, you're likely to lose everything.

This appears to be an uneven game where big corporations get the best advertising results and small businesses struggle uselessly for a more or less satisfying position in Google search results, since they have a tight budget.

In this situation, you have to think of other ad sources that could be more loyal and suitable for such a small business as yours.

1. ExactSeek

    ExactSeek is a flexible advertising platform that allows retailers to attract many visitors to their online stores. It offers various programs from which you can choose the most appealing one.

    Traffic Program. This program requires a quarterly subscription update and seems to be very profitable due to the relatively low cost of advertising services. All ads provided by this program can bring you up to 3,000 visitors during every subscription period. ExactSeek's exclusive traffic-gaining program targets users specifically from the UK, the US, Canada and Australia.

Featured Listings. The program includes Traffic Program combined with simple sidebar ads implemented in search engine result lists and directories. Featured Listings tool offers low-cost investments and prevents you from tracking your ad performance, making additional bids, and inventing too complex advertising schemes.

2. Facebook Paid Ads

    Facebook has its own advertising platform which helps new entrepreneurs with addressing themselves to certain demographics and audiences within a billion-member social community. The principal aim here is to create a separate Facebook profile which will represent your web site inside the social media environment. From there, you can try various advertising schemes to gain the maximum web site viewing results. The main advantage of Facebook Paid Ads is its simplicity and high efficiency.

3. Clicksor

    Clicksor is another alternative to AdWords with targeting certain market segments. It has extremely cheap bidding offers; therefore, you can start investing from just five cents a month. Clicksor relies on time, contextual, and geo targeting to achieve the best advertising results.

4. Yahoo! Bing

    Yahoo! Bing advertising platform is the second most popular service after Google AdWords which has a lot more to offer. If you decide to cooperate with Bing, you can forget about investing in other platforms, since apart from being advertised in Yahoo! Search results, you will get an opportunity to access the service's ad partnership which includes such giants as Amazon and Facebook. Bing is very popular in the US, so you may already know what audience to target there. Moreover, bidding prices are significantly lower on Bing compared to AdWords.

5. Yahoo! Gemini Ads

    This is an additional advertising tool from the Yahoo! search engine with the help of which you will effectively encourage people to visit your web site; but even if conversions remain low, you can be sure that your brand will become more popular than it is now. Gemini Ads works simply: you create an ad and then choose the most appropriate target audience. As always, add a couple of the most relevant keywords and bid for publishing your ad at specific resources.

6. BuySellAds

   BuySellAds is not that popular as the ones described above, however, it is nonetheless effective. It has recently reached a milestone of selling over six billion ads a month; consequently, there are no reasons to omit it. First of all, BuySellAds is aimed at small businesses. It provides convenient ad monitoring conditions, as well as simple and transparent reports that show how your investments are spent. With BuySellAds you can easily monitor your current advertising performance and even pause regular investments in case of an unexpected money shortage.

7. BlogAds

   BlogAds service offers more suitable advertising conditions for certain segment retailers. In fact, with the help of this platform you can advertise your products, using a blog format with various types of ads ranging from banners to custom skins. BlogAds actively cooperates with large blog web sites and social networks that contain easily identifiable target audiences. You should note that monthly prices on BlogAds vary depending on ad placement. The lowest price is about $150 a month.

8. StumbleUpon Ads

   The main advantage of this service is that you can advertise here literally everything you want and still get nice rates of visits. However, numerous visits won't necessarily bring you numerous customers, and StumbleUpon Ads is a place where you can become certain of this statement. Thus, the platform is more likely to be used for getting people acquainted with your brand rather than converting them into buyers.

9. Partner Promotion

   Cooperation among individuals and companies can significantly influence your market presence. Thus, it is often enough to be mentioned in somebody's blog to receive a huge feedback and enlarge the amount of your sales. That's why you should always be sociable and head towards friendship with companies sharing your interest.

Social Media Advertising and SMM campaigns

Social media is still widely used for advertising and sales boost, and it's hard to deny its efficiency in terms of e-commerce retail promotion. With millions of people surfing social network web sites, the traffic source is worth investing. Since different platforms unite people with various tastes and interests, you have lots of opportunities to reach your target audience. Unfortunately, social advertising is no longer free of charge. Sometimes, you will even have to pay as much as you would spend on an AdWords campaign, but there are still lots of opportunities related to this kind of advertising. Start your SMM campaign with the following steps:

1. Clarify your campaign's objectives: increased traffic, engagement, clicks, etc.

2. Choose a right type for your campaign: you can use ads (boosted organic ads for everyone, specific promoted ads aimed at certain user group), share some brilliant content, or combine both approaches.

3. Define your target audience. Luckily, social media provides tons of information about users. Use this data wisely to find your customers and create an approach to uninterested ones.

4. Plan your budget. Set a total monthly budget and calculate a daily budget.

5. Design your ads. Note, that different social networks have different requirements for the content of ads, such as image size and resolution, or a number of characters.

6. Always be on. Note that a quick response can turn your visitor into a buyer.

7. Work with shopping in mind. Socializing is the main reason for people to spend their time on social networks. Therefore, you should pay attention to making shopping better with the help of these services. Sometimes it is enough to add social sharing buttons and enable customer reviews in order to gain maximum profit from social networks. At least, these are core requirements for every e-commerce store. At the same time, you can incorporate social media experience into every aspect of your Magento 2 web site, so don't hesitate to provide your customers with the ability to use their social network profiles everywhere from login to checkout.

8. Combine social media strategy with other marketing strategies. You can always enhance your e-mail marketing template with the help of social sharing options. Moreover, think of utilizing your social media connections to multiply customer subscriptions to your mailing list. And don't forget about Google+ and its influence on search results.

9. Avoid self-serving. Rely on an 80/20 ratio, where 20% is your promotional content, and 80% is the content that engages your customers.

10. Use promoted posts. Usually, such posts don't include any advertising information, drawing users' attention by introducing some truly useful information like how-to guides, interesting facts, digests, photos and videos related to your activity, downloadable e-books, etc.

11. Think of target ads. Using target ads helps you get to a specific social media audience and, as a result, increase web site traffic.

12. Utilize specific social media for specific purposes. For example, business-to-business e-commerce advertising will be more reasonable on LinkedIn; at the same time women-related products can attract Pinterest users. Thus, you should figure out a demographic majority of a social network you're going to use for online advertising.

13. Reward your social followers. Provide them with exclusive offers, bonuses, and discounts. Do you like feeling special? Of course, you do, so why do you think your customers wouldn't like being treated the same way?

14. Social media marketing strategy and visual content:

    • Create eye-catching visual content.

    • Include infographics and video content in your social media campaign.

    • Run video ads with good CTAs[12].

15. SMM and SoLoMo (social-local-mobile technology)

    • Rely on real time engagement to get loyal and highly-active customers.

    • Utilize both offline and online marketing data to track individual and collaborative performance.

    • Reach people with the help of mobile versions of your ads (especially Facebook ads).

    • Use local awareness ads.

    • Try to increase conversions and decrease CPA. Get the lowest possible cost per acquisition.

    • Rely on advanced data insights and social media marketing analysis in a combination with ROI- driven advertising.

16. New platforms

    • Don't limit your SMM campaign to Facebook and Twitter only.

    • Explore your traffic in order to understand where your audience hangs out.

---

[12]https://www.americanexpress.com/us/small-business/openforum/articles/how-to-create-an-unbeatable-call-to-action/

- Learn preferences and tastes of your target audience.

- Don't try to conquer all social networking services.

- Find new social ad channels.

- Allocate budget wisely and reduce wasted ad expenditures.

- Try to avoid using outdated social media tactics.

- Experiment with new platforms and approaches.

In any case, you should analyze the results of your campaign. Thus, you will be able to make vital improvements and fixes and, as a result, enhance its future productivity. It is extremely important to take all your mistakes into account, as well as utilize all past practices. Always try to find answers to the following questions:

- Did you get the expected results?

- What is the ROI of your campaign?

- How did a conversion rate change?

- What are your mistakes?

- How could you improve a future campaign?

Now let's take a look at various social media ecosystems and proven ways of advertising within these ecosystems.

Facebook

Facebook is the most powerful source of online advertising in a social media sphere. Since this network is surfed by all possible users, you can easily reach people who might be interested in products you are selling.

Start with creating your official store page on Facebook. You can do it even more easily by linking your personal page to it:

- Go to Options and select "Create page"

- Choose the most appropriate business category (i.e., local business, company, brand, entertainment, etc.)

- Specify the chosen category to fit your industry type.

- Agree with "Facebook Terms and Conditions" and click "Get Started."

Furthermore, you have to fill your new business page with content. The procedure is quite similar to personal page content management. You should necessarily include a description of your store, create a profile image which might be basically a logo of your company, and add this page to your personal page's Favorites (to get immediate access to it).

Of course, there are several helpful features aimed at increasing the performance of your Magento 2 web site on Facebook. The most reliable ones are described below.

1. Custom Audiences is a handy tool that allows you to monitor those users who come to your web site from Facebook. Moreover, you can even identify which pages they have seen. It is possible due to the aforementioned conversion tracking pixel. With the help of the data gathered by this pixel, you get a better understanding of your customers and their preferences.

2. Lookalike Audiences is another useful Facebook tool that gathers information about the existing customers and utilizes it for searching new users that might be interested in your products.

3. Friend-to-friend Payments is an additional payment method for your store. All Facebook users can now link their debit or credit cards directly to their personal pages and purchase any products right there. As a retailer, you can adjust this feature to eliminate the necessity for your customers to visit your Magento 2 web site and struggle through a standard checkout procedure.

4. Dynamic Product Ads is a library of cool ad templates that considerably simplifies the process of creating ads on Facebook.

5. Multi-Product Ads allows you to display several products in a single ad. It increases your chances to grab the interest of your target audience.

If you still have questions regarding Facebook advertising management, we recommend you look at this profound video-lesson[13] devoted to effective online advertising.

The Best Facebook modules for Magento 2

Facebook covers a vast variety of demographic groups, which can help you build a good stock of loyal audience that always looks for new items on your digital shelves. Utilizing Facebook's endless potential for attracting new customers will become even more effective when you connect your Magento 2 store directly to the social network's features and functions, choosing specialized Facebook modules for Magento 2. Since there are lots of various extensions available for Magento 2, below you will find only those that are really worth being used.

Facebook Store Application[14]

---

[13]https://goo.gl/jZ7j0u
[14]http://www.storeya.com/

This extension offers a complete integration with Facebook as well as an opportunity to customize almost every feature. Developers from StoreYa provided their product with a set of tools that can import all your web site data to a corresponding Facebook page with just one click. Moreover, the module is easy to use, so you won't stop trying to enable or disable a specific feature. Facebook Store Application contains a flexible stats dashboard allowing you to monitor visitors coming from Facebook to your web site, a number of clicks made to get there, and products that tend to be more popular than others. In addition, your Facebook store will be available in all languages, as well as accept transactions in all currencies. The extension is free and adjustable for sharing content across various social platforms.

Twitter

Since this social media network is in second place by the amount of users after Facebook, it is necessary to utilize it for promoting your business as well. Although Twitter shares many features typical for other social networks, it also has a certain amount of unique stuff that makes it more appealing for online advertising. Let's consider Twitter's unique features:

1. Promoted tweets are basic types of ads that require using small input space to attract customers in the most concise way. Thus, you can promote the most relevant products of your web site, the upcoming items of your company, and marketing events you take part in by putting them into a neatly structured tweet.

2. The Promoted accounts feature lets your brand account appear among the leading positions of the Who to Follow list. This will primarily gain more audience to your store and evoke extra interest in your current inventory.

3. Promoted Hashtags are available for the most successful merchants due to high cost. They are placed in the Trends widget in order to make users notice and discuss them in their feeds. Moreover, users often click on hashtags to find all related tweets and discussions.

4. Liking product-related tweets is a pretty smart promotion scheme that allows attracting Twitter users' attention to your brand. For instance, if your business concerns making furniture, you can use Twitter Search to look for users that have your keywords in their posts (like "new bed," "furniture store," "nice wooden tables") and add their posts to Favorites.

5. Twitter Offers is an official Twitter feature that enables merchants to create card-linked promotions and share them with other Twitter inhabitants.

6. Quick Promote Ads. To use this Twitter feature, you need an advertising account. According to it, your tweets will target those users that are interested in your current followers.

Twitter modules for Magento 2

Of course, managing your Twitter profile apart from the web site will not work unless you link it to your store page. Check one of the first Magento 2 Twitter extensions here.[15]

Instagram

Despite Instagram being considered less adjusted for advertising, it still attempts to level up as a competitive social marketing platform. Merchants are now widely using Instagram for posting the photographs of their goods to attract the attention of local users. There are more than 475 huge companies on Instagram. Such giants as Disney, Electronic Arts, The Gap, and Taco Bell implement their ad campaigns with the help of Instagram. This social networking service still lacks real advertising features, but there are already numerous methods created to boost your efficiency on Instagram:

1. Carousel ads is a feature that has recently been launched within the network. It enables merchants to add multiple photographs into one post. Images are simply swiped left, so there are no obstacles for you to grab users' attention. Such brands as Samsung, Banana Republic, and L'Oreal Paris have efficiently used this feature for their campaigns.

2. Specific amount of hashtags adoption. According to recent stats, e-commerce merchants prefer using more hashtags than any other businesses which work on Instagram. The lack of keywords and links is the main reason of such behavior. So don't hesitate to utilize hashtags, but use them wisely.

3. Feedback to your followers is the most powerful action on Instagram because it helps you get more trust and loyalty. An individual approach is likely to bring positive results from your interactions within this social media service.

Instagram extensions for Magento 2

If you intend to make Instagram your primary social media traffic source, you will simplify your goal with specialized Magento 2 extensions developed for the best practices in interaction with Instagram users. We will update this section of the book right after the first Twitter extensions for Magento 2 is published.

Pinterest

Pinterest is a visual content social media network that consists mostly of US users. Another useful demographic fact is the ratio between female and male users: women account for about 80% of all Pinterest users. Moreover, most of these women are in their forties; consequently, you get a sufficiently reduced target audience. But you still have the chance to get new customers here, so don't give up on this network.

---

[15]https://github.com/jasonalvis/magento2-twitter

So what should you do in order to drive more traffic to your Magento 2 web site?

1. Create multiple company boards. Each board can be devoted to a specific type of your product. Additionally, try to utilize more creative, sensitive, and even touching images that are somehow related to your product.

2. Provide short descriptions, direct links, and prices to your item images.

3. Give preference to lighter, taller and no-face images. According to statistics, these tactics boosts the amount of repins to 23%.

4. Place a pin button on your web site to provide your customers with the ability to share your products with their followers.

5. Use both rich pins and promoted pins features for your ad campaign. Although these features are not free, they are rather effective in a Pinterest environment. Rich pins allow you to include additional information about your products including prices, sales, quantity, and brand. Promoted pins are designed to enlarge your audience.

6. Utilize effective hashtags, since there is only one you're allowed to have on Pinterest.

Pinterest extensions for Magento 2

Here[16], you can find all Magento extensions for integration with Pinterest. As for Magento 2 modules, they are not yet available.

Best blogging platforms worth using

If you haven't adapted a blog for your online store yet, check the following list of the most powerful blogging platforms. All the solutions mentioned below will provide you with a full set of features allowing you to maximize customer responsiveness and bring more traffic to your Magento 2 store.

WordPress[17]

WordPress is considered to be the best blogging platform which perfectly suits the needs of e-commerce businesses from any possible niche. The platform is built on PHP and MySQL and is totally open-source, which allows you to implement further customizations to meet the specific needs of each user. The main functionality of this blogging solution is available for free, but if you intend to attract more customers to your store, you might acquire a special business plan for $299 per year. This plan includes

---

[16]https://goo.gl/i43uqN
[17]https://wordpress.org/

unlimited storage space, the ability to create custom links, and access to advanced plugins and additional blog themes.

Movable Type[18]

This blogging solution is aimed at businesses looking for an advanced dashboard to manage their workflow, optimize the level of performed tasks, provide a high-end self-service support, etc. The main advantage of the platform is its ability to create original and outstanding content that is likely to interest your customers. The whole pack of tools and features can be purchased for $595.

Squarespace[19]

The platform offers a unique blogging solution for e-commerce merchants by introducing a mixture of a blog and an online store where you can share information with your customers and at the same time sell your products and services. You can utilize Squarespace's free customizable domain together with paid plans (ranging from $8 to $24 per month). The most expensive plan allows merchants to sell an unlimited number of products through the Squarespace platform.

Typepad[20]

Typepad combines easy-to-use functionality and a set of useful analytics tools which can easily turn your blog into the second main source of traffic. For only $8.95 you will get all the necessary features aimed at the best blogging experience.

Tumblr[21]

Being a smart combination of a micro-blog and a social network, Tumblr offers support for texts, images, and videos. With such content, you can create a perfect environment for merchant-customer interactions. Since it is possible to use all the platform's features for free, you're welcome to utilize all Tumblr's potential for embodying your creative ideas.

Pen.io[22]

Pen.io is an alternative blogging platform that can be used anonymously and absolutely for free. Thus, you don't have to register or pay for using any of the web site's features. Moreover, you're allowed to use your own URLs without any additional domain submission. The platform is fast and user-friendly, so you won't have to waste time on learning how to apply any particular feature.

Weebly[23]

Weebly platform is famous for its multi-purpose functionality, allowing you to create a blog, an online store, or a separate web site. Blogging features include drag-and-drop mechanics, customizable themes, and progressive feedback opportunities. You can start your blog with a basic free plan or you can purchase a more advanced premium plan for $4 per month.

Anchor[24]

---

[18]https://movabletype.org/
[19]http://squarespace.com/
[20]http://www.typepad.com/
[21]https://www.tumblr.com/
[22]http://pen.io/
[23]http://www.weebly.com/
[24]https://anchorcms.com/

It is a useful open-source platform which offers an opportunity to build up custom blogging elements in HTML, JavaScript and SCC. The only restriction is that it works with the latest browser versions, so don't hesitate to update your software. You can get full access to the platform's features for a single donation of $5.

You can find more information about other useful blogging solutions in this article.

Best Magento 2 modules for blogging

Despite the fact that blogging platforms significantly improve the performance of e-commerce projects, they still have one major disadvantage: blogs are detached from the primary online store, which makes it more difficult to interact with customers. That's why e-commerce developers are concerned with integrating blogging features into retail web sites. Magento 2 platform also has a wide range of free blogging solutions which you can use along with your web site.

Blog for Magento 2 by aheadWorks[25]

Since aheadWorks is one of the best and most well-known companies on the Magento market, its extensions are always reliable, user-friendly, and useful. And Blog for Magento 2 is not an exception.

This Magento 2 extension includes all the features dictated by the best industry practices, because it was designed with the ability to create and manage the most engaging content in mind.

When exploring this Magento 2 blogging extension for the first time, pay attention to its feature-rich content editor, which incorporates all the essential writing/design features and tools. A slightly deeper exploration will lead you to the understanding of SEO-friendliness available with Blog for Magento 2 by aheadWorks. All the best practices are implemented within the module. You can easily get SEO-friendly URLs, an XML sitemap, and metadata by using the extension.

Content navigation of this Magento 2 Blog is a separate topic, since it provides one of the most convenient ways of traveling through various categories, tags, and sidebar blocks. If you are wondering, how good are the comment management features of this Magento 2 extension, we can say without any doubt that they are excellent due to the DISQUS integration. Additionally, the extension offers instant live support and clear documentation.

Blog Extension for Magento 2 by MageFan[26]

MageFan also offers a tool which can help you create a professional blog on Magento 2, where your awesome posts will look even better. The extension supports multiple languages, so you can write your posts on any one available on your Magento 2 web site. And with the aid of a convenient search system, your visitors will easily find the materials they are looking for.

To increase views and sales, you can use relinks to your products and other posts as well as add widgets with recent posts or monthly archives. Additionally, there is the possibility to move your posts and even whole categories from WordPress.

Blog Extension for Magento 2 by MageFun is SEO-friendly, since it uses optimized permalinks. As for sitemap XML and RSS Feed, they are also available with the module.

---

[25]https://firebearstudio.com/blog/aheadworks-blog-for-magento-2-and-1.html
[26]http://magefan.com/magento2-blog-extension/

Blog by MageArray[27]

Nobody will deny that blogging is among the best marketing tactics nowadays. That's why running a blog on a Magento 2 web site is among top steps of every pre-launch checklist. And with the Blog Extension by MageArray, you can easily implement all the powerful blogging features on your e-commerce shop. Promote newly launched products, inform your buyers about upcoming items, or just tell interesting stories about your business—the extension offers such opportunities.

With user-friendly category management, you can not only make the navigation on the blog easier, but set metadata per category, improving your SEO. Other SEO features include friendly URLs, meta titles, keywords, and descriptions per post, category, or author, as well as auto generation of Breadcrumb. Additionally, the Blog Extension by MageArray provides the ability to tag posts, so your users can find the desired information with minimum effort.

As for comment management, your clients get the ability to share their thoughts by leaving comments. As a store administrator, you can approve these comments manually or use the auto-approval feature. All spammers will be stopped because of the captcha feature. It is also worth mentioning that MageArray Blog for Magento 2 lets your readers share your post on social media, providing you with new visitors and potential customers.

Blog Pro by Magenest[28]

If you still cannot imagine your Magento 2 web site without a blog, but the aforementioned Magento 2 extensions do not look like the solution of your choice, pay attention to Magenest Blog Pro. It's a powerful and completely open-source Magento 2 extension. Get a great opportunity to communicate with your customers and promote your goods among all visitors of your web site for free.

Note that the Blog Pro extension is integrated into social media services. Hence, readers can easily share your posts on Facebook, Twitter, Google+, LinkedIn, or wherever else without any additional tools. As for navigation, the extension supports categories, so customers will never get lost among your articles, how-tos, and reviews.

In case you would like to find out more about how to integrate your e-commerce project into an online social environment, don't hesitate to read this profound social guide[29] from our team.

Real Time Social Experience with Periscope and Meerkat

Periscope[30] and Meerkat[31] are two new social services designed for real-time streaming. Both solutions can be utilized within any e-commerce business. Below, you will find their features, core differences, and e-commerce opportunities.

---

[27]https://www.magearray.com/blog-magento-2-extension.html
[28]http://store.magenest.com/magento-2-blog-pro.html
[29]https://firebearstudio.com/blog/a-complete-guide-to-the-use-of-social-media-in-e-commerce.html
[30]https://www.periscope.tv/
[31]http://meerkatstreams.com/

Both Periscope and Meerkat produce live streams, which is their core common feature. Another aspect is integration with Twitter, but in the case of Periscope links-sharing is optional, while Meerkat tweets all content automatically. Thus, Periscope users can easily control their audience of viewers.

Another difference consists of the availability of recorded content after the end of your stream. Periscope keeps videos 24 hours, while Meerkat doesn't provide any storing capabilities, which leads to a broken user experience. In addition, Periscope provides more tight integration with Twitter: you get access to your followers right within the app.

Periscope is currently used by such giants as Pepsi's Mountain Dew, Spotify, and DKNY. Starbucks and MasterCard are among Meerkat's prominent users. When it comes to the number of users, Periscope also holds the lead position. But what about e-commerce opportunities?

Since videos have always helped in becoming transparent with customers, live streams play a prominent role in this process. You can easily inform your target audience about any latest offer or product by using social streaming services.

There is also an opportunity to show your business from inside, since you already have lots of customers interested in this information. Moreover, this will help you to get new ones. Note that a live stream is a great tool for establishing credibility among your target audience. You can even stream live demos of your products, which will make your e-commerce business even more attractive. Thus, by providing live lessons related to products you sell, sharing some interesting facts, or offering any other engaging content, you will utilize the e-commerce opportunities of Periscope and Meerkat:

1. Place your customers in the middle of flash sales.

   You can easily engage your customers with the help of Periscope or Meerkat by placing them at the center of a flash sale. You just need to start a live broadcast of your event and make customers communicate with you. This should look like a TV show: your customers are not only situated on your e-commerce web site, they're live on the air with you.

2. Introduce your e-commerce business with the help of Q and A session.

   There are probably dozens of customers willing to ask questions about your business. Don't send them to the FAQ section of your web site because there is a better solution. You can gain their confidence with the help of Q and A sessions. You just need a Periscope or Meerkat live stream. Don't be afraid to show yourself to your customers: by being relatable you will push your e-commerce business to a new level.

3. Build product awareness and grow your sales.

   Ask your customers to add their real-life examples while you broadcast product information. This will not only help with building product awareness, but also increase consumer confidence and, as a result, sales.

4. Provide the customer with better user experience.

   You can utilize live streaming for your customer support needs. Thus, you will be able to provide help not only to a particular customer, but to the whole audience of your buyers.

5. Get real time feedback.

   Ask buyers to leave feedback to your goods and services in real time. You can call them or even invite to broadcasting events. If someone famous is using your products, ask this person to take part in the streaming.

6. Turn all your offline events into online ones.

With the help of both Periscope and Meerkat, you can easily turn all your offline events into online real-time translations. Since you have customers who are not able to take part in your events, you will provide them with such opportunity.

The following tips will help you maximize the effectiveness of your Periscope or Meerkat campaigns:

- First of all we recommend you think about personalization: greet your viewer by nicknames or names; stay polite; don't be afraid to say a name every time you answer a question or address a user.

- Announce your live streams a few days before you go live. You should do this on all possible platforms, as well as on your web site. You can also use eye-catching banners to attract more attention.

- Never omit questions. It's always better to say that you don't know the answer.

- Being in a landscape mode, Periscope still displays messages from your customers in a portrait mode, making a stream inconvenient for viewers. That's why you should use it in a portrait mode only.

- Both Meerkat and Periscope are tightly connected to Twitter. You should always remember this nuance while creating a title for a new broadcast. Use the following hashtags to increase your findability on this social network: #periscope; #werelive; #livestream; #livebroadcast.

Social influencers for promoting your products online

One of the most up-to-date methods of gaining some traffic to your web site is dealing with famous people on the Internet. They include media personalities, bloggers, vloggers, and even social media accounts run by different people all over the world. All of them are perfect as marketing channels to boost sales on your web site. This marketing technique might be particularly interesting for those who have recently launched their business, but now suffer from the shortage of traffic.

1. Get to know some Instagram influencers.

    Instagram is now very popular among younger audiences, and it may become crucially tempting to attract new customers from such a crowded place. Moreover, it was found that Instagram is the platform giving 25% more customers to those brands that integrate their products with the local influencers than any other social media networks.

    So, if you intend to find influencers for promoting your online store on Instagram, start looking for primarily those accounts that specialize in activities that might be directly or indirectly connected with your goods or services. The common mistake in this case is to look just for the most popular users with a great amount of followers. It's more likely that you will tap into a community that has nothing to do with your web site at all.

    To make your search even more productive, use a handy web site called WEBSTA that keeps all the popular Instagram hashtags and user information in its database. Users with an impressive amount of followers usually don't limit themselves by having only their Instagram page. Probably, they have their own web sites and blogs. Meanwhile, Instagram plays the role of an additional promoting source. Having found several potential candidates, don't forget to look at their bio or contact page. Web site links and e-mail addresses are the main indicators of the fact they don't mind cooperating with e-commerce businesses.

    Another way to target influencers on Instagram is through the official mobile app. You can basically browse "the popular page" with thousands of the most popular photos in search of those that somehow relate to your business. Through them you can reach the owners of those photos and contact them through e-mails (if possible).

    The final thing is to write to the chosen Instagram account holders to attract their attention to your web site and its products. You basically have to write a letter, which must be as neutral and loyal as possible, saying that you're a fan of a person and his or her posts, and you've just launched your own web site dedicated to the things you're selling. Further, you should kindly ask a person to try a sample of one of your products and share it with his or her followers. At the end, you can attach one or two images of your product. Alternatively, you can just leave a link to your web site page.

2. Look for popular YouTube vloggers, bloggers, and press.

Like Instagram, YouTube is full of popular users, and, what is more important, they don't mind promoting stuff which is not only a part of their target subject but also stuff that is not related to their subject at all. To reach out to the appropriate vloggers, you can use the native search engine of the web site by typing keywords that describe your business interest. The same traffic-gaining strategy is applied for bloggers, but can be realized through the Google main page. It's worth noting that targeting bloggers with less followers is often more profitable than targeting those with thousands of them since a small audience is usually more loyal to its blogger, his content and advertising than a big one.

As for the press, you might have paid more attention to local news sites rather than global ones. Here, however, you have a chance to promote your products only by writing about them in the most original way and presenting it as a good pitch: laconic and interesting to read. So if you want to grab the attention of the press, make your story concise and valuable.

3. Do some smart advertising on Reddit.

This platform is very useful in terms of its mechanics, which allows you to get involved with an appropriate user category right through a corresponding thread called subreddit. There are thousands of subreddits devoted to every possible subject, so you're likely to find what fits you the best. But the thread which must be of the utmost importance to you is always in "/r/entrepreneur" subreddit. There you will find a lot of useful discussions concerning business and ways to improve it. "/r/smallbusiness" is another option for new entrepreneurs.

If you managed to find a subreddit dedicated to your web site content, you can post unobtrusive little sentences there containing a nice and catchy offer to purchase your products for satisfying user needs. However, if you exaggerate with this offer, you'll probably be banned. That will bring you no actual profit. Therefore, read general and/or local Reddit rules first.

4. Convert your family and friends into customers through Facebook.

Making advertising posts on your Facebook page seems legit and, what's more important, free. Moreover, this way of attracting customers is one of the first free online advertising methods being adopted by thousands of businesses all over the world. It might not bring you much profit after all, but you shouldn't lose the opportunity of making a few customers out of the people you know. You can even make a 50% discount for them: allowing your friends and family to behave as special customers can make them become loyal buyers, after all.

5. Extend your web site to Twitter * It's also a good idea to create a separate Twitter profile for your web site, but it's certainly not enough for getting more traffic to your web site. * The initial strategy in this case is the same: use appropriate keywords and find people posting tweets about content related to your web site. * The next step is to follow those people, as they might become interested in what you're doing. * Take part in your product-related events such as fairs or presentations; make sure you post a tweet with cool photos. * Inform your followers about new stuff coming out—keep their interest warm.

6. Mention your potential influencers in a profound blog post.

This method might become one of the most effective ones, as it's probably going to get through to target influencers' hearts. The only thing you need to do is to write a blog post about their activities combining all the information you have under a unified title and catchy introduction. When writing about their blogs, don't forget to mention their names, because this is what will make a good job for your web site.

Amazon Product Advertising

There is nothing more reasonable than advertising on Amazon since this is the biggest and the most popular e-commerce platform that ever existed. It's no surprise that the company works hard on allowing merchants to fulfill their marketing ambitions in the easiest way. However, if you want to turn your web site into the primary destination for Amazon users, then Amazon Product Ads is what you really need to utilize.

In general, Amazon Product Ads is a program for external businesses selling their products outside the Amazon platform, which plays the role of a product promoter attracting more customers. How to start using it?

1. Create Amazon Product Ads account here[32]. If you already have one account, simply sign in on the same page.

2. Then you can go to the "Settings" bar and select "User Permissions." Here, you will get a pretty long list of product, advertising, report, and additional settings which you have to either check or uncheck depending on your preferences. Save the changed permissions.

3. Complete your account information. Go to "Settings > Account Info."

---

[32]https://services.amazon.com/content/sell-on-amazon/sponsored-products.htm

4.   Set a daily budget by clicking on the corresponding category in the "Advertising" bar. The daily budget setting page is rather straightforward, which means that you can set only one price for all your ads on Amazon.

5.   Then you're able to upload a product list file by selecting "Add Products via Upload." In the new window click on "Download Template." You will have to choose the most convenient template format here.

6.   Amazon Product Ads requires using the following attributes: category, title, link, SKU (stock keeping unit), and price. Thus, you should be ready to edit your uploaded product feed according to the requirements above.

7.   After you have uploaded your product feed, wait while it is processed. You should also check Status Report for errors.

8.   Later, when you decide to change the bidding amount or update your inventory, you will have to upload a new product feed to Amazon Product Ads. Seems tough, but if you find Amazon helpful, it's the only way to get the maximum from the marketplace, since there are no alternative solutions.

Keep in mind that every SMM campaign is unique. Try to figure out all the particular proprieties of your e-commerce business in order to create the most effective social media strategy. You can rely on third- party social media companies, hire a social media marketer, or do everything with the help of existing specialists. It's up to you, but core principles of a successful campaign will always be the same.

CHAPTER 14

■ ■ ■

Security

Although Magento is the safest e-commerce platform, there are still additional security tricks, which make it even safer. Thousands of Magento web sites have been hacked during the last few years. Luckily, there are several useful methods developed to fix all the major problems. Below, we'll tell you about the most important security tips. You can check whether your storefront is secure and unaffected on `MageReport.com`.

1. Name & Password

   You should make all your Magento passwords unique and strong. The same is true about an admin name. This simple step will help you improve the security of your web site. Just create a password which is longer than eight characters, and to some extent you will prevent your store from being hacked. Note that passwords should combine numbers, letters, and special characters. Indeed, do not use weak usernames such as 'admin' or 'administrator'. If you are using an insecure name and password, you can always change them in "System > My Account."

2. Custom Path for Admin Panel

   A default path to an admin panel has the following construction: "`http://storename.com/admin`." Everyone knows it, consequently it is among Magento's security vulnerabilities. By changing it to a more complex path, for example "`http://storename.com/superadmin`," you push the security of your e-commerce web site to a new level. This small step is the best defense against Broken Authentication/ Session Management Attacks.

   You can always change the Magento admin path in the "app/etc/local.xml" file. Find the line which contains "<![CDATA[admin]]>" and create a new string instead of admin, for instance "superadmin." The new code should look like the following: "<![CDATA[superadmin]]>".

© Viktor Khliupko 2017
V. Khliupko, *Magento 2 DIY*, DOI 10.1007/978-1-4842-2460-1_14

3. Two-Factor Authentication

    Another reliable security technique is a two-factor
    authentication. It adds an additional security layer
    to an existing one. The system requires two separate
    authentications to provide users with access. Thus, your
    Magento web site becomes two times more secure. You can
    provide your admins with the two-factor authentication
    solution using Two-Factor Authentication by Xtento[1].

4. Encrypted (HTTPS/SSL) Connection

    One more essential security improvement is the usage of
    the HTTPS/SSL secure URLs. Being HTTPS/SSL-encrypted,
    your e-commerce web site will be PCI-compliant as well. It
    means that you will get a secure data transfer between your
    site and server. Otherwise, there is a risk that data (database
    information and login details) will be intercepted by hackers.

    To enable the HTTPS/SSL secure URLs, you should go to
    "System > Configuration > General > Web." Then, it is necessary
    to change 'http' to 'https' in the Base URL, and enable the "Use
    secure URLs for both Frontend and Admin" feature.

5. File Upload with Secure FTP

    In addition to the HTTPS/SSL secure URLs, you can also take
    care of the FTP connection with your server. Use SFTP, since
    it provides an additional encryption of user credentials. This
    protocol uses a private key file for authentication. Make sure
    that file permissions are not set to 777. Otherwise, anyone will
    be able to rewrite them.

6. Predefined IP Addresses for Administrators

    Magento provides an opportunity to set predefined IP
    addresses for accessing the admin panel, which is a robust
    security enhancement. You just have to create a list of IPs;
    thus, users with other addresses won't be able to access the
    admin panel of your web site.

    To implement this security feature, find your ".htaccess" file
    and enter the following code into it:

```
1   AuthName "Protected Area"
2   AuthType Basic
3   <Limit  GET POST>
4   order deny,allow
```

---

[1]https://firebearstudio.com/blog/xtento-two-factor-authentication-for-magento-
2-and-1.html

```
5    deny from all
6    allow from 172.161.132.13
7    allow from 153.119
8    </Limit>
```

Hence, you will implement a permission to access your admin panel for the user with the '172.161.132.13' IP address, and for everyone whose IP address starts with '153.119'. This technique supports an unlimited number of IP addresses.

Then, you should go to Magento root directory and create a new folder called 'admin'. Copy the "index.php" file of your Magento and paste it there. Now, you have to change relative paths to the "config.php" and "Mage.php" files. Change the lines below:

```
1    $compilerConfig = '../includes/config.php';
2    $mageFilename = '../app/Mage.php';
```

You should only add '../'.

Now go to the ".htaccess" file and enter the following lines:

```
1    Redirect permanent /index.php/{admin_path} /admin/index.php/{admin_path}
2    Redirect 301 /index.php/{admin_path} /admin/index.php/{admin_path}
```

Therefore, you will direct users coming to our admin to a new directory. '{admin_path}' indicates a new admin path manually changed before.

This security step works only with static IP addresses. If your ISP assigns dynamic IP addresses, you shouldn't implement this technique.

7.   Malicious PHP Functions

There are malicious PHP functions that should be disabled. You can use more secure alternatives instead of them. To disable these functions, find your "php.ini" file, open it, and add the following code:

```
1    disable_functions = "apache_child_terminate, apache_setenv,
     define_syslog_variables, escapeshellarg, escap\
2    eshellcmd, eval, exec, fp, fput, ftp_connect, ftp_exec, ftp_get,
     ftp_login, ftp_nb_fput, ftp_put, ftp_raw,\
3    ftp_rawlist, highlight_file, ini_alter, ini_get_all, ini_restore,
     inject_code, mysql_pconnect, openlog, p\
4    assthru, php_uname, phpAds_remoteInfo, phpAds_XmlRpc, phpAds_
     xmlrpcDecode, phpAds_xmlrpcEncode, popen, pos\
```

```
5   ix_getpwuid, posix_kill, posix_mkfifo, posix_setpgid, posix_setsid,
    posix_setuid, posix_setuid, posix_unam\
6   e, proc_close, proc_get_status, proc_nice, proc_open, proc_terminate,
    shell_exec, syslog, system, xmlrpc_e\
7   ntity_decode"
```

Take into account that you can disable other functions in your "php.ini" file, as well as omit important functions from the code above.

8. Directory Listing

Directory listing is among common server loopholes. It provides everyone with the ability to see the directory structure and location of all its files by simply entering a web site's URL. Therefore, you should disable directory indexing by adding the code below to your ".htaccess" file:

```
1   Options -Indexes
```

9. MySQL Injections

Since every Magento web site has lots of form fields for user data input, hackers can easily steal this data by injecting MySQL statements. To protect your store from such a threat, you should use web firewalls (several apps are described below).

To solve this problem, update your Magento to the latest version, as it always provides lots of improvements, bug fixes, new features, and security enhancements. At the same time, there is a possibility of popping up new undiscovered problems related to the latest update.

10. Create backups of your Magento store regularly. It will help you decrease every hack damage level, and you will be able to restore your Magento web site faster.

11. Fix all e-mail loopholes. Keep in mind that your e-mail should not be widely known. It should be protected by a unique and secure password as well.

12. And don't forget to check the security of your Magento web site regularly. This will help you find all issues at early stages.

13. Always update your antivirus software, since its older versions are not able to protect your store from the latest threats.

14. Find out where your browser comes from, as it stores lots of necessary information about your Magento web site. Try not to save passwords in it because, with the access to your computer, hackers will easily get your credentials.

15. The "local.xml" file contains such sensitive data as database information and encryption key. Hide it from public access. You can do it by changing file permissions for "local.xml" to 600(-rw) or blocking a web access to the entire app directory.

16. Upgrade your OS to the most recent version. It should provide new security improvements.

17. Your hosting provider should be reliable and secure. Note that some hosting providers are not prepared for hacker attacks.

18. Provide limited permissions for files and documents. For downloadable documents set only read permissions, thus no program will be able to modify them.

19. Disable Magento Connect Manager after having installed extensions in order to prevent any random changes.

20. Use only trusted Magento extensions from reliable sources, such as Magento Marketplace.

21. Change passwords for outside developers. You can set your ordinary passwords back after work is done.

22. Check web server logs for errors or suspicious activities. Thereby, you will be able to detect threats at early stages.

23. Block unwanted countries if you are not shipping worldwide.

24. Check this PDF[2] for more tips. Although it was written for Magento 1, you will find a lot of information useful for Magento 2 there.

25. And don't miss the first Magento 2 security extensions[3].

---

[2]https://goo.gl/CqvYd6
[3]https://firebearstudio.com/blog/magento-2-admin-login-security-extensions.html

CHAPTER 15

Certified Partners

© Viktor Khliupko 2017
V. Khliupko, *Magento 2 DIY*, DOI 10.1007/978-1-4842-2460-1_15

Passing through a series of tests is not an easy task, but it's the only way to become a Magento 2 Trained Solution Partner. And there are several companies which already have this status. Therefore, we've decided to create the following list of Magento 2 Trained Solution Partners.

Inchoo

Inchoo is one of the top Magento 2 Trained Solution Partners. There are 20 Magento Certified Developers and 11 Magento Certified Solution Specialists among the company's members, who are ready to support demand for Magento 2, all tested by Magento in back-end and front-end development. Follow the link below for further information.

Inchoo is a Magento 2 Trained Solution Partner.

Alpenite

Another company which has the final achievement for the Magento 2 Beta Partner Program is Alpenite. Its portfolio already has an e-commerce store based on Magento 2 EE. Unfortunately, we don't know about the quantity of certified specialists among company's employees. Under the following link, you will find more information.

Alpenite has received the official "Magento 2 Trained Solution Partner" status.

Forix

Forix is also proud to be a certified Magento 2 Trained Solution Partner. The company has operated on the e-commerce market since 2009, and the certification is a great step in its development.

FORIX ACHIEVES MAGENTO 2 TRAINED CERTIFICATION

Session Digital

Session Digital is the UK's largest Magento partner that works with both global retailers and local merchants. Being a Magento 2 Trained Solution Partner, it can help your brand make a smooth transition to the second version of the platform. For further information, examine the link below.

Magento 2 migrations and upgrades

Briteskies

The Briteskies company also has the badge of a Magento 2 Trained Partner. After completing the Magento 2 Trained Partner Program, the company published an article about the course on its web site. You can check it here:

How We Survived the Magento 2 Certification Process

Space 48

Space 48 is also among the first approved Magento 2 Trained Solution Partners. You can see this news on the official web site of the company. Besides, you will find the Magento 2 Trained Solution Partner badge there as well as other of the company's achievements.

MAGENTO 2 TRAINED SOLUTION PARTNER

More than 80 companies from around the world have completed all Magento requirements to become Solution Partners. You can find a full list of developers here.

CHAPTER 16

■ ■ ■

Final Thoughts

Since it is the early days of the platform, the book you've just read introduces only basic aspects of Magento 2. Therefore, we are going to release several more editions of Magento 2 DIY to cover more features and details. The platform is rapidly growing, providing us with new opportunities every month. Thus, 2016 will be one of the most interesting years from the perspective of Magento merchants, developers, admins, and marketers. For further information about Magento 1 and Magento 2, visit Firebear Blog[1].

---

[1]https://firebearstudio.com/blog/

© Viktor Khliupko 2017
V. Khliupko, *Magento 2 DIY*, DOI 10.1007/978-1-4842-2460-1_16

Index

Get the eBook for only $4.99!

Why limit yourself?

Now you can take the weightless companion with you wherever you go and access your content on your PC, phone, tablet, or reader.

Since you've purchased this print book, we are happy to offer you the eBook for just $4.99.

Convenient and fully searchable, the PDF version enables you to easily find and copy code—or perform examples by quickly toggling between instructions and applications.

To learn more, go to http://www.apress.com/us/shop/companion or contact support@apress.com.

Printed in the United States
By Bookmasters